THE
SALEM WITCH TRIALS

Gallows Hill, Salem, Mass., 1949

CONTENTS

GALLOWS HILL, SALEM
On the morning of June 10, 1692, the first woman in the Salem witch trials died by hanging. Until 2016, it was believed to have been on this infamous hill. Scholars and researchers have now determined that the victims were hanged in the shadow of this hill, on a rocky crevice known as Proctor's Ledge.

INTRODUCTION

THE CLIMATE OF FEAR: THEN AND NOW

In the past, witches were those accused of Satanism who stood apart from society. Today, the role of the outsider has evolved

By Carina Chocano

"**W**itch hunt," that newly trending phrase, has undergone a particularly Orwellian inversion in recent years. Since the middle of the 20th century, when the playwright Arthur Miller turned the Salem witch trials into an allegory for McCarthyism in *The Crucible*, we have used the term to describe a particular kind of persecutory campaign against a vulnerable, marginal or unorthodox minority in which the false accusation is wielded like a sentence. By contrast, the term "witch hunt," as introduced by Miller into the cultural lexicon, has always been a legitimate counter-accusation. It identifies and names this fraudulent practice, thereby exposing it to the light of reason and justice.

Lately, in the kind of tactical misdirection favored by despots and totalitarian regimes throughout history, "witch hunt" has been reimagined, usually by men in positions of power, as a rubber shield against any accusations of wrongdoing, no matter how legitimate, sourced and well-grounded. Reversals like these don't happen by accident. In George Orwell's novel *1984*, "Newspeak" eradicates meaning by inverting it, replacing it with a Manchurian version of itself. Something similar has been happening with the repetition of "witch hunt." The more it's misused, the more firmly it establishes an alternative "illusory truth" much like the one it was coined to puncture in the first place. This is what makes its co-option so scary. It defuses our ability to expose abuse by recasting the exposure *itself* as abuse.

This method of turning reality on its head is the whole point. It's a means to evade responsibility. Even in their earliest, literal incarnation, witch hunts were about power—and ideological control. From the Würzburg witch trials to the Moscow Purge Trials, moral panics have always been about using faith, patriotism, morality or ideological purity as cover for power grabs and the suppression of dissent. Scapegoating is a handy way to create a climate of fear, the kind of fear with no solution that leads to submission. It's a classic brainwashing technique:

the "fright without solution." Witness that notorious witch trial of observing an accused in water: sink, you're not a witch, but dead; swim, you're a witch, and sentenced to death. This is the double bind we find ourselves in today.

WHAT IS A WITCH? AND WHO

gets falsely accused of being one, or whatever we've swapped in as the modern equivalent? It depends on whether we're talking about the newly fashionable holistic healers and occultist dab-

COURTING DISASTER
Between 1936 and 1938, Joseph Stalin orchestrated a series of trials to eliminate any opposition within the Communist Party. Here, Konstantin Semenchuk and Stepan Startsev are sentenced.

blers or about our moral scapegoats. These days, a (reclaimed) witch can be a cute, blue-haired girl on Instagram posting pictures of her crystals and her motivational spells. Or she can be a pretty, magenta-haired spell caster writing an essay for a beauty magazine, like the self-described modern-day witch Sophie Saint Thomas, who declares: "If you feel an urge to exert your will and get what you want (while fighting the patriarchy and practicing intersectional feminism), you qualify" as a witch. In other words, the term "witch" can be proudly or playfully reclaimed, because other scapegoats have taken witches' place.

In medieval Europe, around 80% of people accused of being witches were women. In those pre-Victorian days, women were thought to be the morally weaker, more sexually voracious sex—and as they got older and found fewer sexual partners, they became more susceptible to being seduced by the devil. Women branded witches tended to be on the older, poorer side and more autonomous and outspoken. Often they were midwives, who could be seen rushing around under cover of night to deliver babies, whose occasional deaths were blamed on them. They were cooks and healers with knowledge of medicinal herbs, which they could turn into healing remedies or harmful poisons. Libidinous spinsters and widows were threatening enough to the moral order, and God help them if they had opinions. The sharp-tongued or foulmouthed lady of a certain age, the ill-tempered scold or quarrelsome neighbor was almost guaranteed to invite an accusation. So were nonconformists, bad housekeepers and ladies with vivid imaginations. In other words, take any contemporary television show about city-dwelling single women and transpose it to the 16th century, and it's almost certain that every one of its characters would be tried, convicted and executed before the end of the first season. I can only thank my lucky stars I was born when I was. After reading Anna Garland's "The Great Witch Hunt: The Persecution of Witches in England," her legal history of witches and witch hunts published in 2003 in the *Auckland Law Review*, I have no doubt that I would qualify.

Garland explains that before the 15th century, beliefs about witches in England coexisted on two separate planes. There was a popular belief in witches' ability to perform *maleficia*, or evil deeds, as well as to fly. Peasants blamed witches for a wide range of misfortunes and bad luck—illness, failed crops, the death of a cow. But the upper classes, the Catholic Church included, did not believe in these powers. They considered these ideas to be mere folktales and superstitions, holdovers from a pagan past that Catholic priests sometimes still incorporated into their rites and rituals.

It's a common misconception that the Catholic Church created the hysteria that surrounded witches, Garland says. The preconditions for witch hunts were

CHILDBIRTH TRAGEDY
This religious miniature
depicts the death of Rachel,
the Old Testament wife of
Jacob, who died in childbirth,
surrounded by nursemaids and
female attendants.

> The sharp-tongued lady of a certain age, the ill-tempered scold or quarrelsome neighbor was almost guaranteed to invite an accusation.

— △ —

always more cultural, legal and even geographical than strictly religiously motivated. Witches were persecuted following the Crusades, and then after the Norman expansion made contact with Eastern religions, and then following the Black Death and the religious tensions of the Reformation era. It's as if in times of turmoil and uncertainty we have always allayed our anxieties by taking them out on people who seem different. Even when cloaked in hysteria, the religious and political powers that be have never stopped availing themselves of witch hunts as a means of consolidating power. The endgame of a witch hunt is always to eradicate difference and impose a single ideology.

The first major witch trials, in Switzerland in 1427, established that witches were "magical practitioners owing their evil powers to a pact that they made with the Devil." The papal bull of 1484 denounced witches as evil and gave the thumbs-up and go-ahead to witch hunting. Shortly thereafter, two enterprising inquisitors published *Malleus Maleficarum*, or "The Hammer of Witches," which legitimized witches for those who hadn't believed in them. It also served as a handbook for judges and magistrates in identifying and punishing witches, running 20 editions. By the 15th century, Garland wrote, "it became accepted knowledge among theologians that witches were not isolated individuals dabbling in the occult, but rather members of a demonic, anti-Christian heretical sect." In other words, it was not that witches were a threat to other people so much as they were a threat to Christianity that really got the hunts going. Witchcraft didn't become a crime in England until 1542, during the Protestant Reformation. In a Manichean world in which everything was broken down into good or evil, witches were relegated to the wrong team. They were a threat to the patriarchal order.

Women were not the only ones accused of being witches (20% were men); as New Advent's *The Catholic Encyclopedia* points out, *Malleus Maleficarum* "was sensational in the stigma it attached to witchcraft as a worse crime than heresy and in its notable animus

against the female sex." The more authoritarian and patriarchal the context, the more likely powerful, independent, outspoken women, especially if they were older, would be branded as witches. This is a recurring thread in American politics to this day. Who can forget Bernie Sanders's supporters' charming chants of "Bern the Witch" in reference to his opponent? Or the 2010 *Wizard of Oz*–themed campaign ad in which then-Speaker of the House Nancy Pelosi was portrayed as the Wicked Witch of the West, a role that U.S. Senator Kamala Harris has also been cast in?

THE SALEM WITCH TRIALS—THE FIRST BIG American witch hunt, which took place in 1692—was distinctly American in several ways. First, they took place in Salem Village—a very small, agrarian community addled by economic anxiety. Furthermore, the Puritans were misogynists. Women were expected to be silent, submissive and confined to the home. They were not allowed to be ministers. They were thought to be more likely by nature to enlist in the devil's service than a man was.

The village was not incorporated and relied on

the much bigger, more cosmopolitan Salem Town for commerce, government and access to ports. In "Religiosity and the Political Economy of the Salem Witch Trials," published in 2010 in *The Social Science Journal*, historians Ernest King and Franklin Mixon Jr. note that Salem Town was wealthier and more secular than Salem Village, "which wanted to operate as a theocracy." Salem Town relented in letting the village operate its own church, but West

Salem Village's choice of minister led to tensions with the richer and more cosmopolitan East Salem Village.

One colonist, Anne Hutchinson, who resided in Boston 56 years before the events at Salem, had evolved ideas about the rights of women, was openly critical of the church and held Bible studies in her home that were popular with other women. As the accusations of 1692 began, they mostly consisted of West Salem Villagers accusing East Salem Villagers. Those worried about protecting themselves from witches started filling the church, which meant the minister made more money. Most of the accusers were young girls, most of the accused were older women, and most witnesses at the trial were married. Some believe the witch trials were used to maintain the status quo. But there were other things at play. "That the Salem ministers used the hysteria to effect an increase in the demand for salvation is also consistent with earlier work in this genre … which suggests that [Samuel] Parris and the other ministers exploited the young female accusers for personal and corporate gain," King and Mixon write. "In other words, there was a market for ministers to sell religious services to members of the community, and to acquire and maintain market share."

Hutchinson was among those brought to trial, condemned and banned from the Massachusetts Colony.

MODERN DEPICTIONS
Top right, in 1939's *The Wizard of Oz*, Dorothy faced off against an evil witch with Glinda, the good witch, running support. Above, Macbeth and the Weird Sisters in Shakespeare's *Macbeth*.

She was, in a sense, lucky: many others who faced similar censure during the Salem witch trials were sentenced to death. And, as ever, the motivation for the persecution of truth seems to lie at the end of a trail of money. *Plus ça change.* ▲

European Origins

A widespread moral panic engulfed parts of Europe during the early modern period. Those accused of witchcraft were depicted as Satanic worshippers intent on reducing their communities to ruin

SOURCE OF POWER

ON MAGIC, WITCHES AND WITCHCRAFT

Whether it was white, black, high or low, premodern Europeans
believed firmly in the existence of magic

By Matthew Plunkett

n the Middle Ages, everyone knew witches were real. Male or female, they were practitioners of high or low magic. Some were midwives; others, astrologers or alchemists. To the average European before the Enlightenment, the existence of magic was a fact of life.

Part of this was that most people didn't have a modern understanding of science, which meant that belief in the supernatural dominated so many facets of life. That could mean unusual occurrences in the natural world or cases of human suffering and death. In the Judeo-Christian tradition, the witch first appears in the Books of Exodus and Deuteronomy. In those texts, the witch simply represents a being who is intent on opposing the existing power structure of society. Despite the explicit condemnation of witches in the Pentateuch, premodern Europeans largely viewed witches as a nuisance to be managed, although they distinguished between good (white) magic and malevolent (black) magic. Those seen as possessing magics that helped people (often, women and men with medical knowledge) were forgiven for consorting with forbidden knowledge—at least at first.

Magic is "a power that is activated and controlled by human beings themselves . . . to produce readily observable, empirical results in the world," according to Brian P. Levack, a historian who has written extensively on witches and witchcraft. And in those days, it was viewed as unequivocally real. Individuals such as midwives who employed their powers for beneficial acts practiced "white magic." Acts of white magic might include curing an illness or assisting crops to grow. But for every act of good existed an equivalent act of malevolence. Black magic, or *maleficia* that was "intended to bring about bodily injury, disease, death, poverty or some other misfortune," included such terrors as the death of a child or livestock.

Class and gender played significant roles in how magic was categorized. Divination, astrology and alchemy, typically practiced by those with an educated background, are cited as examples of high magic. Magicians or witches who practiced high magic were largely drawn from the upper echelons of society and included folks such as Sir Isaac Newton (alchemy) and Galileo (astrology). Not surprisingly, these men (and they were nearly all men) were deemed useful for society and, as such, rarely faced persecutions.

FLYING TO THE SABBATH
A common medieval belief, captured in this 18th-century painting by A.F. Saint-Auber, supposed witches flew through the night sky to cavort with the devil at a witches' Sabbath.

Low magic, on the other hand, required no formal education. Often passed down through apprenticeships and oral traditions, low magic typically took the form of simple charms and spells. Of course, all acts of black magic were categorized as acts of low magic, clearly echoing existing biases of social stratification. Simply put, the poor and uneducated were more likely to be considered witches, while the rich and the educated were allowed to practice a "higher form" of magic undisturbed.

Gender played a key role in the European witch hunts. Although some men stood trial for witchcraft, the vast majority of victims were female. Historians estimate that across Europe, women accounted for nearly 80% of those accused and convicted of witchcraft between 1450 and 1750.

A common belief in medieval Europe considered women both "morally weak and sexually charged," says Levack. Women's lack of moral character and unchecked lust left them more susceptible to the diabolical charms of the devil. These theological beliefs painted a dire picture among the educated elite, resulting in high numbers of women accused of witchcraft.

Among the common folk, however, it was women's roles in society that more often led a witch hunter to their door. In premodern Europe, women bore responsibility for the preparation of meals and often served as healers and midwives within the larger com-

SUSPECT OF HERESY
Above, the astronomer Galileo addresses his heresy before members of the Vatican in 1633, captured in a 1847 painting. Opposite, Jean-Baptiste le Prince's *The Necromancer.*

munity. These jobs provided greater opportunity, according to the beliefs of the time, for women to employ magic to act maleficently toward others. Cooking and healing required the gathering of herbs and imparted the skill to transform raw ingredients into something magical. If the potion failed to heal the sick, then perhaps witchcraft was to blame. A midwife's role in the mystical and misunderstood process of childbirth provided plenty of opportunity for a woman to face charges of sorcery if either the mother or the child suffered. Levack highlights the belief in witches sacrificing infants to the devil during the Sabbaths as another reason midwives—and their ability to procure babies—fell under suspicion.

Women's weak position in society, lacking both physical and political power, offered a final explanation. Magic gave women the means to enact revenge or punishment for perceived wrongs or injuries they could not otherwise pursue. Levack wrote that "the power to bring about harm by magical means was one of the few forms of power that were available to women in early modern Europe . . . By having her tried and executed, her neighbors were not simply picking on a helpless old woman but counteracting a form of female power that had placed them, their children and their domestic animals in considerable danger."

In a life full of danger and death, the citizens of premodern Europe often turned to magic to help remove some of the uncertainty of the world. Tragically, the ubiquity of this belief did little to protect the vulnerable in society when attitudes and fears evolved.

TOWARD THE END OF THE MIDDLE Ages, particularly as the 15th century unfolded, a shift in mindset began to take hold, moving citizens from tolerating witches and the use of magic to persecuting them. The definition of a witch began to evolve, reflecting the fears and attitudes of an increasingly Christian society. No longer was a witch solely someone who committed acts of *maleficia*. Instead, a witch was understood to be someone who both committed *maleficia*

> Magic could give women the means to enact revenge or punishment for perceived wrongs or injustices they could not otherwise pursue.

— △ —

and had a pact with, worshipped and attended nocturnal meetings with the devil.

According to Levack's 1997 book, *The Witch-Hunt in Early Modern Europe*, those three key convictions about witches swept through Europe and the British Isles. These preconceptions of witchcraft, which evolved over time and took centuries to fully develop, were helped along by the leadership of the Catholic Church, which worried about apostates corrupting its faithful congregations.

Descriptions of the Sabbath varied, but had common themes: witches performed sacrifices, ate children and infants and copulated with demons.

— △ —

Witches, under this new worldview, received their power directly via a pact with the devil, and in exchange they were granted the ability to perform *maleficia* toward others. They supposedly rejected their Christian faith in an initiation ceremony led by the devil and consisting of dark, offensive rituals. In some versions, it was a baptism performed by the devil himself, during which either the devil placed a distinctive mark on the woman's body, he engaged in sexual intercourse with her, or the woman paid homage with the infamous obscene kiss, in which she kissed the devil's buttocks. With the ceremony complete, the woman then received specific instructions about how to perform her dark tasks.

The average European also believed that witches, both male and female, gathered with other witches at nocturnal meetings, called the Sabbath. These meetings might draw hundreds or thousands of witches, all of whom received the power of flight by the devil in order to travel great distances for the celebrations. Descriptions of the Sabbaths varied in the telling, but a few common themes repeated: witches performed sacrifices, occasionally ate children and infants and copulated with demons or even the devil himself. Because of these gatherings, it became widely understood that witches could fly. Some early Germanic superstitions around strigae, supernatural beings that would transform at night into screech owls, also evolved into the witches' backstory.

Without widespread belief in the Sabbaths, the larger witch hunts that swept Europe might not have taken place. No longer, after all, was a witch a solitary figure. If a community discovered a witch, its members understood there to be a confederation, or coven, of witches yet to be uncovered. The local authorities would be forced to expand their search for additional witches, transforming a once-discrete trial to a wider inquiry.

As in most aspects of witchcraft, small regional variations existed on the activities that allegedly took place during these nocturnal meetings of witches. Universally, however, the Sabbaths reflected an inversion of the moral and religious norms of the culture. Cannibalistic infanticide, a nearly universal human taboo, and naked dancing

A JOURNEY IN ANIMAL FORM
The witches gather on Walpurgis night. The Christians of Germany prayed to Saint Walpurga, a German 8th-century abbess, for protection against witchcraft.

were common descriptions. Other activities sometimes reflected the specific fears of medieval Christianity, such as the heavy emphasis on the erotic (copulation with the devil; promiscuous fornication among the participants). According to Levack, Sabbaths sometimes mocked specific aspects of the Catholic service, including "the saying of the Nicene Creed backwards while the celebrant stood on his head ... the consecration of a host made of offal, turnip or some black substance, and the singing of the choir in 'hoarse, gruff and tuneless voices.'"

THE SPREAD OF KNOWLEDGE about witches in the 15th century advanced in two different ways: public witch trials resulting in confessions, and written treatises on the subject of

WITCH FINDERS
One of several notorious witch finders, Konrad von Marburg, pictured at center in robe, sends an accused witch to the torture chamber—and eventually to the stake.

witchcraft. Confessions extracted from suspected witches, often through the use of torture, would be read aloud in a public space.

But it was that technological marvel, the printing press, that helped spread a number of scholarly texts to various judges and religious leaders combating the threat of witchcraft. Of all the treatises concerned with witchcraft, one text stands out for its impact on codifying the threat of witches into a coherent narrative. The story of how it came to be written begins with a decree from the pen of Pope Innocent VIII in December 1484:

"It has recently come to our ears, not without great pain to us, that in some parts of upper Germany ... many persons of both sexes, heedless of their own salvation and forsaking the Catholic faith, give themselves over to devils male and female, and by their incantations, charms, and conjurings . . . ruin and cause to perish the offspring of women, the foal of animals, the products of the earth."

Pope Innocent VIII issued the above papal bull in response to a request from Heinrich Kramer and Jacobus Sprenger, two Dominican inquisitors responsible for ending witchcraft in parts of Germany. The bull authorized Kramer and Sprenger "to exercise their office of inquisition and to proceed to the correction, imprisonment and punishment" of any witch found. Armed with their new divine mandate, Kramer and Sprenger renewed their efforts and together wrote *Malleus Maleficarum*. Completed in 1486, *Malleus Maleficarum*, translated as "The Hammer of Witches," stands out in a crowded genre for what historian Elspeth Whitney described in 2005 as "its single-minded insistence that witches were the source of evil in the world."

Described by historian John Demos as "part bible, part encyclopedia, part operational guide," *Malleus* provided judges and inquisitors a primer on how to deal with the supernatural threat. In their text, Kramer and Sprenger drew a direct line between witches and the devil and outlined specific evil acts performed by these servants of the devil.

Most historians believe that the bulk of *Malleus* was written by the hand of Kramer, with Sprenger brought on as a co-author to lend an added layer of intellectual and spiritual authority. In truth, *Malleus* stemmed from Kramer's lifetime of, in the words of historian Hans Peter Broedel, "vigorous, zealous and uncompromising war against enemies of the faith."

By 1485, Kramer was the most experienced inquisitor in Germany, and by all accounts, he was a learned scholar, having earned a prestigious doctorate of theology from Rome. He was not popular among his peers; nearly everyone who interacted with Kramer found him abrasive, arrogant and nearly impossible to work alongside. A bishop in Innsbruck, as quoted by Demos, described Kramer as "a senile old man." The charge of senility was unfounded, despite Kramer's advanced age when he began writing *Malleus*. His mind was sound, but one can rightly label him zealous or eccentric in his single-minded pursuit of heretics.

In his text, Kramer cited his experience prosecuting more than 200 witches in the years leading up to the publication of *Malleus*. In all likelihood, that number is vastly overstated. As Broedel points out in his 2003 work, *The Malleus Maleficarum: Theology and Popular Belief*, there

Malleus Maleficarum provided judges and inquisitors a primer on how to deal with the supernatural threat— and drew a direct line between witches and the devil.

— △ —

is scant historical evidence that Kramer took part in more than a few witch trials. Even the few trials with surviving documentary evidence show that Kramer's inquisitions experienced significant resistance from the local secular and religious authorities. Broedel points to lack of cooperation as one of the primary factors that pushed Kramer to write *Malleus* in the first place.

In addition to furthering the view of women as "more ready to receive the influence of a disembodied spirit" and possessing "slippery tongues . . . and, since they are weak, they find an easy and secret manner of vindicating themselves by witchcraft," the authors of *Malleus* offered up many quotations to support their misogyny. From Ecclesiastes 25: "I had rather dwell with a lion and a dragon than to keep house with a wicked woman. All wickedness is but little to the wickedness of a woman." From the Roman playwright Terence: "Women are intellectually like children." From the early-5th-century archbishop of Constantinople, St. John Chrysostom: "What else is woman but a foe to friendship, an inescapable punishment, a necessary evil, a natural temptation, a desirable calamity, a domestic danger, a delectable detriment, an evil of nature, painted with fair colours!"

Malleus pushed the church's argument further by stating that the devil targeted women because they were "more carnal than a man" and "all witchcraft comes from carnal lust, which is in women insatiable." The inherent weakness of women, a so-called by-product of the use of a bent rib in her very formation by God, left her in a position of subservience to man. According to the logic of witchcraft, this provided women with the motivation to pursue, as historian Jessica O'Leary puts it, "diabolical magic to increase their power." Envy naturally drove women to embrace witchcraft.

MALLEUS MALEFICARUM INSTRUCTS ITS READERS how to examine, sentence and (eventually) execute women suspected of witchcraft. But most important, the text argues for the prosecution of witchcraft in a secular, not a

The blending of the folk and the theological, as well as the papal authority claimed by *Malleus*'s authors, helps explain why the book grew to become the most influential witch-hunting guidebook in Europe.

— △ —

theological, court. After all, the authors reason, the crimes of witchcraft have real consequences to persons and property and should be considered the same as any other act of vandalism or assault and thus prosecuted by the state. The arguments laid out in *Malleus* served to accelerate this shift toward the use of secular courts in the elimination of witches—which eventually came into play during the events in 1692's Salem Village.

EMERGING ONLY 50 YEARS AFTER GUTENBERG'S invention of the printing press, *Malleus* was the first witch-hunting treatise to reach a wide audience, and it benefited greatly from that new technology. Its functional, matter-of-fact advice on the best practices for bringing an accused witch to trial helped local inquisitors all across Europe and the British Isles to prosecute and punish witches in secular courts.

Despite the book's popularity, second only to the Bible for multiple years, historians note that *Malleus*'s publication did not coincide with a surge in witch prosecutions in Europe. In fact, despite its multiple reprintings, nearly 30 years passed before the next wave of witch hunts in Europe. However, during the intervening years, the concept of a witch as laid out in *Malleus* grew to become the widely accepted definition among the learned of Europe. Historian Broedel argues that this was due to the alignment between the commonly accepted vision of a witch and the definition laid out by Sprenger and Kramer. This blending of the folk and the theological, as well as the papal authority claimed by Sprenger and Kramer, helps explain why *Malleus* grew to become the most influential witch-hunting guidebook in Europe.

During that time, the information and arguments laid out in *Malleus* seeped into the global consciousness, helping to standardize and normalize the torture of those accused of witchcraft and the use of secular courts to try them, and helping to inspire the witch-hunters who led the inquisitions of future generations. ▲

TRIALS AND TRIBULATIONS
The Dutch painter Willem de Poorter captured this trial in the early 17th century. The largest trial in the Netherlands took place in 1613, where 64 people lost their lives.

Inside the Book

Malleus Maleficarum established familiar witch lore, but some of its more preposterous claims are still pretty wild

---

After its initial publication, numerous editions of *Malleus Maleficarum* were published in Latin, with German, English, Italian and French translations in later centuries. As printing presses improved, copies of *Malleus Maleficarum* began featuring detailed illustrations depicting—in addition to gruesome methods for witch detection and torture—witches in action, whether cavorting with the devil, blighting cattle or cooking children for consumption. The images were based on the text, which described some fairly outlandish witch behavior, like witches using a magic ointment to fly on broomsticks (the book wasn't the first mention of that activity, but it helped codify it) or performing the *osculum infame* ("shameful kiss"), an illicit act wherein witches would commit to Satan by kissing his posterior . . . very literally. *Malleus Maleficarum* even included some cautionary tales for men about witches who filched penises to keep as living pets or to secret away in birds' nests and boxes. —*Nancy Lambert*

THE BURDEN OF PROOF

INSIDE THE WITCH TRIALS

In the 16th and 17th centuries, roughly 40,000 to 50,000 people were executed in Europe for witchcraft. Here's how

By Matthew Plunkett

Ask any American to describe the appearance of a witch and most will respond with something resembling the Wicked Witch of the West from the 1939 movie *The Wizard of Oz*: dressed in black, with a mean narrow face, a pointy black hat, a broomstick, maybe even that green face. Most telling: nearly all descriptions will be female. Although the magicians of early Hollywood produced the popular conception of a witch, their handiwork was firmly grounded in historical context. As the writers of *Malleus Maleficarum* (the essential witch-hunter's manual during the witch hunts of the 16th and 17th centuries) reminded their readers, some are flawed creatures too weak to repel the advances of the devil, yet simultaneously carnally insatiable and deceitful.

Not all witches were women, but women received the lion's share of witchcraft charges. Historian Robin Briggs, author of the landmark work *Witches and Neighbours*, writes that women were three times as likely as men to face execution (subject to significant regional variation). Precise numbers for the 16th and 17th centuries are notoriously difficult to ascertain, but many historians believe 40,000 to 50,000 individuals were

executed in Europe on the charge of witchcraft, with men making up roughly 20% of the total. While viewing witch hunts as women-hunting does not fully explain their phenomenon, Briggs argues that pointing to external forces like patriarchalism can oversimplify their tragedy.

When seeking answers to an issue that stretches across an entire continent for a period of nearly two centuries cannot be done—at least definitively—historians are able to sketch a picture of what made a "typical" witch—and why they were prosecuted. Tellingly, the typical woman accused of witchcraft was both far older and far poorer than her neighbors. Some historians estimate that half of these women were widows, many without any surviving children. A society that believed in witchcraft would look to those isolated from the rest of the community, like a poor widow or a childless woman, when seeking outside explanations for misfortune.

WIZARDS AND WITCHES
A colored woodcut by the artist Hans Schaufelein in 1512 depicts a man surrounded by devilry. The *Malleus Maleficarum* was published just 25 years earlier.

WHILE THE BELIEF IN WITCHCRAFT is ancient, the shift from belief to persecution through organized witch hunts developed only after four significant changes took place—all occurring between the 13th and 16th centuries.

> Even though witchcraft became a secular crime during this period, the punishment meted out to those convicted remained that of a heretic.

— △ —

The first major shift occurred in the court system in Europe, which affected the ecclesiastical and secular courts. Prior to the adoption of this new, inquisitorial system, the courts utilized an accusatorial procedure—a system that relied on nonrational ordeals and appeals to the Almighty. For example, an individual would start a judicial procedure by making a sworn accusation in front of a judge, and if there was any doubt about the guilt of the accused, the court would subject the accused to an ordeal and await a sign from God. A typical ordeal might involve having the accused hold a hot coal in his hand while walking a certain distance. After a few days, the accused's hand was presented to the court for interpretation. Any sign of a wound was understood to be a sign from God of his guilt. But if the accused was found innocent, the accuser faced criminal prosecution—a large deterrent to submitting to the courts at all.

By the 13th century, European courts had shifted toward an inquisitorial system of criminal procedure, in which a judge or jury was responsible for gathering and evaluating the evidence and determining guilt or innocence. In addition, anyone filing an accusation no longer faced criminal charges if the accused was found innocent. As a result, the courts effectively removed any "liability of the accuser" and opened the door for denunciations of suspected witches with impunity for the accuser.

Another key change in the court system, which occurred during the same period, was the authorization of judicial torture. While torture was used in ancient Greece and Rome (and later at various times in the early medieval period in Europe), its reintroduction in the 13th century was predicated on the belief that the application of pain would force a victim to speak the truth. Significant restrictions were created to limit torture's duration and severity and when it might be applied, all with the goal of eliminating false confessions. In practice, however, these restrictions were loosened—or entirely ignored. Many jurisdictions appeared to save the most heinous torture precisely for accused witches. And sadly, historian Brian Levack notes, "once the torture was begun, judges had an additional motive for completing their task successfully, since the confession itself served as justification of their use of torture in the first place."

A third evolution of the judicial process was the increased role of the secular court in the prosecution of witches. Ecclesiastical courts quickly gave way to their secular counterparts. As written in *Malleus*, there was a legal argument for viewing witchcraft as a secular crime (primarily viewed as the destruction of property). However, not until the 16th century were anti-witchcraft laws written in nearly every European country. This shift also coincided with a steady erosion of papal authority in the wake of the Reformation.

It's an interesting note that, even though witchcraft became a secular crime during this period, the punishment meted out to those convicted remained that of a heretic. With the exception of England and New England, where witches were hanged, most European witches were sentenced to burn at the stake. John 15:16 provided the biblical foundation for this ritual: "If a man not abide in me, he is cast forth as a branch, is withered; and men gather them, and cast them into the fire, and they are burned." In addition to acting as a purification ritual, the burning of a witch assured a nervous community that she would not return from the dead. Contrary to popular belief, however, witches were typically not burned alive. The authorities in France, Germany, Switzerland and Scotland usually killed the convict prior to the flames actually consuming the body. Spain and the Italian territories were the exception to this rule.

Finally, local jurisdictions were given the independence to prosecute witches directly throughout most of Europe. While the central authorities did not abdicate all power, the majority of witch trials were initiated and prosecuted in the courts of the local manor, town or province. These local courts typically proved significantly more zealous in their prosecutions of witches than the more removed central authorities. The fear of having a witch among the community fueled the prosecutions, and local prosecutors and judges were given largely free rein in their witch hunts.

WHEN THE EUROPEAN WITCH HUNTS BEGAN IN earnest, two clearly different types of persecutions emerged. The first, a localized trial of witchcraft, typically featured an accusation of a single witch. Those isolated cases followed a familiar pattern: resentment and anger built up in small communities over years or decades. If an event of misfortune or suffering occurred to one party, then it was possible, with enough time and repeated misfortune or quarrels, to raise witchcraft as the cause. When

a formal accusation was made, a large group of witnesses would provide testimony, and the suspect would be formally charged, arrested and committed to prison, where the accused would be searched for the "devil's mark."

The trials would then commence, and the evidence from the witnesses would be recounted before a verdict would be reached. As historian John Demos highlights, the primary charge was *maleficium*; only occasionally was the charge of diabolism leveled. Once the trial concluded and the punishment meted out, the balance within the community would be restored.

At the other end of the spectrum were full-blown witch hunts. The distinguishing factor between the two is simply one of scale. A witch hunt might begin with an individual

case that grew to include others. But it was often initiated by the appearance of a formal "witch finder," typically a member of the clergy trained to flush out suspected witches from a community. In the latter case, the mood in a community would be panic. Accusations (and counter-accusations) rolled in fast and furious, particularly after a confession. And, yes, there were confessions: with the use of judicial torture on the table, witch finders nearly always found a witch.

Confessions brought forth additional names in a spiral of fear as the charges shifted from mere *maleficium* to the far more serious diabolism. The motivating factor appeared to be the fear that all of Christendom was under attack from the devil and his legion of demons. Inquisitors focused their questions on the interactions with the devil, particularly those that occurred during the nocturnal Sabbaths.

In the end, these witch hunts petered out for a number of reasons. Demos theorizes that "sheer exhaustion" likely played a role, as did the sense from authorities that the panic had gone far enough. If and when the accusations began to name prominent members of the community, as happened later in Salem, authorities often took steps to shut down the hunt.

THE GREAT EUROPEAN WITCH HUNTS WERE NEI-
ther a singular event nor carried out in the same manner across the continent. Significant regional and temporal differences marked the prosecution of witches. An outbreak of witch prosecutions in the north of France, for example, might occur 50 years before

a similar outbreak in southern Germany. Likewise, the focus on gender varied widely across Europe. In Iceland, almost 90% of the charges were brought against men. France, on the other hand, witnessed near parity between the sexes. Within a specific country, the gender equity of the charges was also marked by tremendous regional variations. In the regions of northeastern France, women made up the vast majority of witches, far more than in the central and western portions of the country.

Individual witch trials took place over centuries throughout Europe. One of the more famous trials was that of Dame Alice Kyteler of Kilkenny, Ireland, who stood accused of both practicing sorcery and heresy in 1324, making the trial one of the first in which someone stood accused of the combined charges. Such trials took place in nearly every region of nearly every country throughout the continent and the British Isles over

THE EXECUTION
Below, witches in England meet their end by hanging. Opposite, the 16th-century Anabaptist Anneken Hendriks faces death by fire after a trial by the Spanish Inquisition.

the next several hundred years. However, it was a 70-year period that is most associated with the term "witch hunt." While this series of isolated witch hunts all shared a number of common features and motivations, each event was also shaped by local forces.

Historians largely agree that the peak of these witch hunts took place roughly between the 1580s and 1650, although there were some outliers. (Southwest Germany witnessed a spike in witch hunts in the 1560s, and Sweden's did not occur until the late 1660s and early 1670s.) The north-central region of Europe, comprising much of modern-day Germany, Switzerland, northeastern France and the southern Netherlands, was ground zero for European witch hunts. This region contained less than half of Europe's population yet accounted for three quarters of the convicted witches.

Witch hunts skyrocketed during different decades, often due to economic pressures, such as the shift to commercial agriculture, which placed significant strain on the peasant class, including dislocation and dispossession for many. Outbreaks of plague and famine and the climatological upheaval caused by what historian Brian Fagan has dubbed the Little Ice Age all served to disrupt society. The continent also faced constant upheaval in local peasant revolts and religious conflicts between Catholics and Protestants. In the face of such calamity and uncertainty, it is perhaps no wonder that people sought to affix blame for their collective woes on the "witches" in their midst. And, of course, the European colonists crossing the Atlantic en masse took their superstitions and irrational fears with them, setting the scene for the tragedies to occur once more. ▲

MAJOR EUROPEAN WITCH TRIALS

Amid centuries of gruesome European witch hunts, these five trials stand out for their notable size, scope or brutality, and sometimes for the combination of all three

By Nancy Lambert

THE NORTH BERWICK WITCH TRIALS
Scotland (1590–1592)

Relying heavily on vicious torture to extract confessions, Scotland's prolonged period of witch trials was sparked by a prominent case overseen by—and involving—Scotland's King James VI (later, England's James I), who had become convinced that witches were behind the particularly turbulent storms that had plagued his voyage home with his new bride, Anne of Denmark. The man who was blamed for coordinating this attempted assassination by sorcery, Francis Stewart, was eventually acquitted. However, the other accused (approximately 70 women and men) were not so lucky; nor were the estimated 3,000 to 4,000 other Scots who were garroted, hanged or burned at the stake in the surge of lower-profile witch trials during the 150 years (1560 to 1707) that included the North Berwick trials.

THE BASQUE WITCH TRIALS
Spain (1609–1614)

Though nearly 7,000 women, men and children were accused of witchcraft during the Basque trials in northern Spain, ultimately only 11 of the accused died (five died in prison, and six were executed in an auto-da-fé witnessed by 30,000 spectators). As panic grew in the region, spurred by rumors of a he-goat-shaped devil leading mass gatherings of witches, a skeptical Spanish inquisitor, Alonso de Salazar Frías, was assigned to oversee the trials. He investigated the confessions of thousands of the accused but found no evidence of witchcraft and dispatched 1,800 cases. In 1614, two years after Salazar reported his findings, the Supreme Council of the Spanish Inquisition (which had always been skeptical of accusations of witchcraft) finally issued a new set of rules to control how local courts could prosecute witches, effectively ending witch hunting in Spain.

CONFESSIONAL TOOL
Burning at the stake was probably the best-known torture technique used on accused witches. But leg screws, like this one from Germany, could also be effective.

THE BAMBERG WITCH TRIALS
Germany (1626–1631)

One of four massive witch trials that terrorized Germany in the late-16th and early-17th centuries (Trier, 1581–1593; Fulda, 1603–1606; and Würzburg, 1626–1631), the Bamberg trials were orchestrated by Johann Georg Fuchs von Dornheim, the so-called Hexenbischof ("witch-bishop"). Fuchs von Dornheim was so obsessed with witch hunting that he created a Witch Commission and erected a dedicated witch prison to contain so-called witches—and then tortured and executed hundreds of people. Ultimately, it was the influential husband of accused witch Dorothea Flockhlin whose appeals to Catholic officials eventually resulted in Fuchs von Dornheim fleeing Bamberg (although not in time to save Flockhlin), and the accused who had remained imprisoned were freed.

THE TORSÅKER WITCH TRIALS
Sweden (1674–1675)

At the peak of Sweden's brief but bloody witch panic, Laurentius Christophori Hornæus, Torsåker parish's priest, used children's testimony—obtained through coercion and torture, such as putting them in an oven and threatening to light it, whipping them and dunking them into a hole in a frozen lake—to accuse about 100 villagers of witchcraft, including his own mother and aunt. Most of the men were freed, and then on one bloody day, the remaining 71 victims, primarily women, were put to death, beheaded and burned. Horrifyingly, the witch hunters were careful to behead the accused away from the firewood so it would not be soaked in blood and still could light. Torsåker's mass execution of accused witches was one of the largest ever recorded in a single day, and it wiped out about a fifth of the region's women.

THE SALZBURG WITCH TRIALS
Salzburg (1675–1690)

The last European witch hunt resulting in at least 200 deaths, the Salzburg trials, also known as the Zaubererjackl ("Magician Jackls") trials, were also notable for targeting young men and boys instead of women. Prince-Bishop Max Gandolf von Khuenburg fixated on Salzburg's gangs of mostly male beggars and their leader, Paul Jacob Koller, a.k.a. "Magic Jackl," after Koller's mother purportedly accused him of witchcraft during her own trial for sorcery (for which she was executed in 1675). Koller evaded capture and execution, but he purportedly died out of custody. Unfortunately, by the time news of his death arrived to government officials, they had redirected their attentions to Salzburg's poorest and most vulnerable. A great witch hunt swept in beggars, homeless and teenagers. The majority of those executed were children and teenagers. ▲

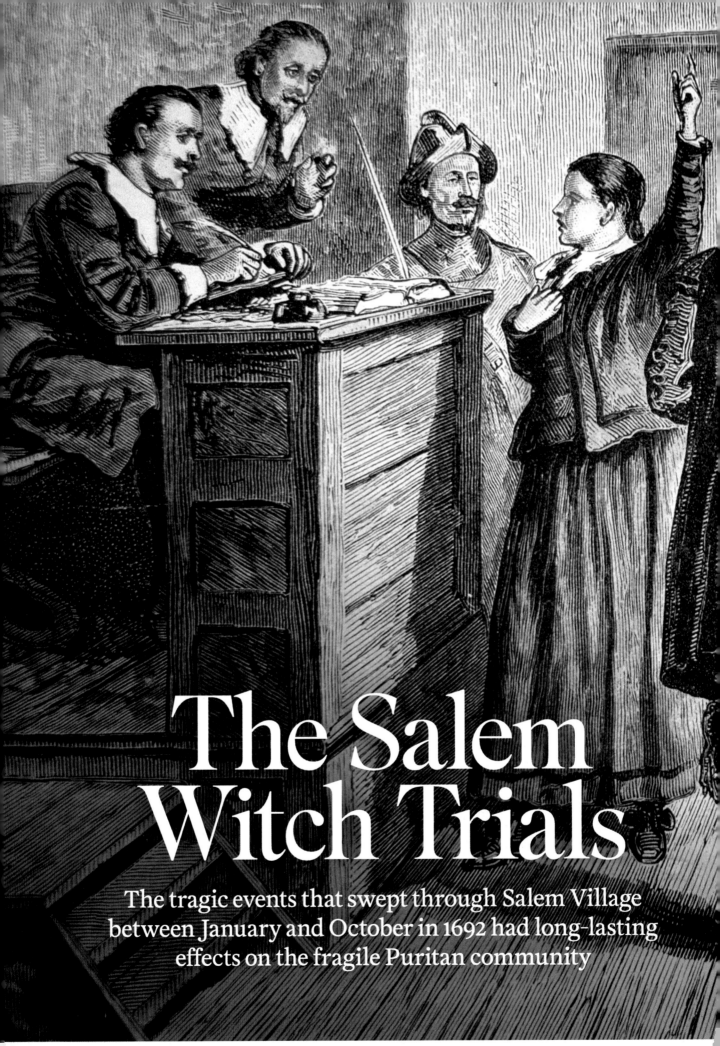

The Salem Witch Trials

The tragic events that swept through Salem Village between January and October in 1692 had long-lasting effects on the fragile Puritan community

A DIVINE MANDATE

PURITAN ROOTS

The European settlers of the Massachusetts Bay Colony brought with them a unique mindset and belief structure that reflected their religious convictions—and an unwavering understanding that if anything went ill, it was because they deserved God's wrath

By Matthew Plunkett

The first wave of migration of Europeans to North America coincided with a surge of witch hunts across Europe, so settlers were already on the lookout for signs of witchcraft when they arrived in the colonies.

After all, no matter their country of origin, these individuals brought with them a host of baggage, both seen and unseen. Alongside their worldly possessions, individuals and families carried to the American colonies their spiritual beliefs, including their deeply held convictions about witches existing as ready instruments of the devil. Much like these European immigrants, the devil was no longer content to remain behind in the Old World. In fact, he did not even wait to reach American shores before rearing his head.

In 1654, Mary Lee, an English settler, boarded a ship in London and set sail for a new life in the colony of Maryland, according to historian John Demos in *The Enemy Within*. At some point during the passage, Lee became the target of rumor among the sailors for allegedly being a witch. At first, the ship's captain held firm and prohibited a trial from taking place. Soon the ship ran into foul winds that threatened its safe passage, and the captain could no longer hold back the collective fear of his crew. Abandoning the deck of the ship for his cabin below, the captain left his men to their own devices. The sailors stripped Lee, discovered what they believed to be the mark of the devil on her skin and proceeded to hang her to ensure the safety of the entire ship.

Lee wasn't the only passenger on such trips to suffer this fate. Threats of "bad weather, sickness, confining conditions, uncertainty about the future, and real danger in the present" set the stage for onboard witch hunts. Those sailing to the Americas sought explanations for their misfortune and blamed witches when their fortunes and the seas turned.

No matter where they landed in North America, European settlers bore their prejudices with them. Though the fear of witches was nearly universal regardless of country of origin, religious fervor in the Protestant-majority colonies of New England was far stronger than in areas like Maryland, with its predominantly Catholic populace, says Demos.

While Virginia recorded the colony's very first documented witchcraft trial, in 1626, by and large the middle colonies did not experience many trials. Demos notes that while the prosecution of witches took place all across the colonies, from Pennsylvania to New York to

THE DEFIANT WOMAN
Anne Hutchinson, shown here on trial, was an outspoken spiritual adviser who openly challenged the Puritan church. She was banished from the Massachusetts Bay Colony in 1637.

> The Puritans believed God chose select people for salvation ("the elect") while condemning the rest of humanity to eternal damnation.

— △ —

the Scandinavian colonies in the Delaware Bay, the official response to early incidents was lukewarm, reflecting the society's waning concern with witchcraft, already nearing its end in Europe. New England, on the other hand, experienced a much more intense relationship with witchcraft, with far more disastrous consequences.

The first witch trial in the New England colonies took place in Hartford, Conn., in 1647. Few details survive to explain the charges against Alse Young, yet she was tried, convicted and hanged for witchcraft, and her execution kicked off a period of intense witchcraft activity throughout New England. Leaving aside the outlier of Salem, the two decades following Young's hanging saw a significant spike in New England witchcraft prosecutions. More than 30 jurisdictions, stretching from Connecticut to Maine, held more than 50 witch trials, resulting in the execution of 11 witches.

THE PURITANS' LONG HISTORY WITH WITCHCRAFT stretched to their origins in England. "Puritanism in England was essentially a movement within the established church for the purifying of that church," said historian Bradford Smith, "for ministers godly and able to teach, for a simplifying of ritual, for a return to the virtues of primitive Christianity." Tied to the timing of the larger Reformation, which began in 1517 with Martin Luther's Ninety-Five Theses, Puritanism sought an end to what followers viewed as the political and spiritual corruption of the Church of England. Much like Luther's attempts to reform the Catholic Church, Puritans wished to "purify" the Protestant Church of England.

Neither Catholics nor Protestants were fond of folk magic, but the belief structure and worldview of the Puritans reserved special scorn for any hints of the supernatural. The Puritans who founded the Massachusetts Bay Colony in 1630 were strict adherents of the teachings of John Calvin, a French-born reformer. Calvin, who believed in predestination, taught that God was all-powerful and mankind was merely sinners. God chose select people for salvation ("the elect") while condemning the rest of humanity to eternal damnation. Yet no one, including the Puritans in Massachusetts, knew whether he or she belonged

PILGRIM SETTLERS
Church of England Separatists (a sect of Puritanism) left Delft Haven, Denmark, on their *Mayflower* voyage to America in July 1620.

to the elect or was destined for punishment. As such, a Puritan's life was filled with spiritual fear and a nearly constant search for a sign of God's favor—or his wrath.

At the same time that these internal struggles took place within each individual, there existed a tension for the soul of the entire community. Like the Israelites of the Old Testament, the Puritans believed they were a chosen people bound to God by a covenant. The collective behavior of the community determined whether they honored that covenant and basked in God's grace or sinned and faced his punishment.

The Puritans left behind in England a series of unprecedented changes. Rapid population growth, economic turmoil and the sprawling chaos of cities, such as London, coupled with the

RELIGIOUS FREEDOM
Above, a preacher offering the first Thanksgiving sermon in the New World in 1621. Opposite, Mary Dyer, a Puritan turned Quaker, headed to the gallows for defying Puritan law in 1660.

Puritans' spiritual doubts (chosen for salvation or damnation), fueled their obsession with control. Their deep religious faith brought security and certitude in an unforgiving and dangerous world; neighbors would keep watch over the actions of one another to ensure the spiritual protection of the whole. The Puritans believed that any one person's deviation from God's path could condemn the whole community to suffer a collective punishment.

Even the most pious and spiritual of the Puritan faithful were occasionally bound to succumb to temptation—after all, anger and envy are part of the human condition. To the Puritans, however, those emotions were interpreted as signs of God's displeasure with the individual and the larger community. Suddenly witches provided an out. When blaming a witch for a feeling of jealousy, Puritans could shift the blame from an individual's spiritual weakness to an external source. Similarly, the failure of a farmer's crops or the illness of a child was therefore not the result of mistakes by the individual but the maleficent act of an outside force: a spiteful witch. In a way, witches purified the community in the eyes of God. By ridding the community of a witch, Puritans were able to retain a clean spiritual slate and reinforce their special covenant with God.

IF THE MINDSET AND BELIEF STRUCTURE OF THE Puritans was unique among American colonists, their conceptions of who might be a witch echoed those of their European roots. Witches accused by Puritans rose from within, typically found in other Puritan families rather than those on the outside of society, such as the Quakers, Catholics or Jews. As always, the average witch was middle-aged and female; married or widowed; and with fewer children than was typical at the time. Much like their European ancestors, Puritan witches often rose from the lower end of the socioeconomic scale and sometimes possessed a history of criminal charges, perhaps for slander or cursing. Finally, and not surprisingly, these women usually possessed a reputation for having "contentious," "obnoxious" or "quarrelsome" behavior.

Reputation and gossip played a large role in the Puritan witch hunts. As in Europe, individuals accused of witchcraft in the colony possessed reputations throughout the community for their ill temper over the course of many years. With no printed periodicals available in the colony at the time (save one short-lived newspaper), news traveled exclusively from person to person. Gossip quickly became fact, and reputations were built over successive years to the point where one's identity became bound with the stories told by the community.

Much as the profile of the accused fit the typical European witch, so, too, the accusers shared the traits of their Old World counterparts. Broadly speaking, accusations were likely to come from one of three groups of people: middle-aged women who might be facing their own loss of status, particularly around reproduction,

Reputation and gossip played a large role in the Puritan witch hunts. With no printed periodicals available, news traveled from person to person.

— △ —

in the community; adult men stressed about beginning a life of their own, starting a family and managing a farm or business; and teenage girls, who existed in a powerless state in society—too young to marry, too old to coddle and often feeling unnecessary and overlooked in their families and communities. Each of these groups possessed a motivation to deflect blame or attract attention. Accusing someone of witchcraft became an easy way to manage their anxieties or release their frustrations about their societal status.

Nearly all European immigrants to the American colonies believed in witches. Yet the peculiarities of the Puritan belief structure, including their strict adherence to Calvinist doctrine, helped set the stage for the tragedy to unfold during the events of 1692. ▲

WHO'S WHO

Often fictionalized in popular plays and films, these are the real people behind Salem's most turbulent and tragic period, from the political players to the wrongfully accused

By Nancy Lambert

BETTY (ELIZABETH) PARRIS AND ABIGAIL WILLIAMS

The first two girls "afflicted" by witchcraft, cousins Betty, 9, and Abigail, 11, led the accusations against Salem's residents and shocked the town with bizarre symptoms, like barking and screaming fits. Betty's father sent her away soon after her "bewitchment" began, but Abigail stayed, ultimately indicting nearly 60 neighbors.

TITUBA, SARAH GOOD AND SARAH OSBORNE

Tragic fates awaited the trials' first three victims. Samuel Parris's slave Tituba avoided execution by confessing, but unable to pay her jailer's bill, she remained imprisoned for more than a year until an unknown buyer purchased her from Salem Gaol. The courts condemned Good and Osborne when they refused to confess. Osborne died awaiting execution, and before Good was hanged in July, she gave birth to an infant, who died in prison. Her 4- or 5-year-old daughter was also convicted as a witch and sent to jail.

REV. SAMUEL PARRIS

Salem's new minister moved to town with his family a few years before the trials and preached frequently and forcefully about the devil's hold in Salem, priming residents for the coming hysteria, which he then continued to fuel from both the pulpit and the witness stand, testifying nine times.

INCREASE MATHER AND COTTON MATHER

Prominent ministers, the father and son wielded political sway in Massachusetts and abroad that proved influential during the trials. While Increase helped install Governor William Phips, who expedited the deadly trials, Cotton's writings on possession and his letters to the judges informed Salem's court proceedings. It was Increase, however, who finally cast doubt and helped end the trials in October.

JUSTICE SAMUEL SEWALL

Appointed by Governor Phips to the Court of Oyer and Terminer, Sewall was one of nine judges to convict and sentence to execution 19 victims. Sewall later expressed deep remorse for his involvement in the events that occurred—the only judge to publicly do so. In a statement, he asked both "pardon of men" and "prayers that God will pardon [my] sin." ▲

ON THE STAGE
A 1957 French production of
The Crucible, or *Les Sorcières
de Salem*, starring Simone
Signoret as Elizabeth Proctor
(far left) and Yves Montand
as John Proctor (far right).
Both Proctors were accused
of witchcraft.

THE CALAMITY BEGINS

THE SALEM WITCH HUNTS

The tragic events that began in January 1692 and ended in October the same year had a major fallout in the already-fragile Puritan community

By Matthew Plunkett

Within the span of 15 months, the legal proceedings around the Salem witch trials swept up at least 144 people, secured the confessions of 54 individuals and led to the execution of 20. Of those, 14 women and five men were hanged and one man had his chest crushed by rocks. The hysteria and the accusations reached far beyond the geographic limits of Salem Village, eventually engulfing more than 20 towns and villages in the vicinity. Unlike in previous witch trials, the accusers named people they did not intimately know and did so at a rate not seen before in the colonies. It remains one of the most shocking and studied episodes in American history.

The outbreak of fear began in Salem Village, an offshoot community of Salem Town. Salem Town was the first permanent settlement in Massachusetts Bay Colony, settled in 1626, but as its population grew, families moved outward to claim land in the surrounding country. Salem Village was the smaller, more conservative farming community that existed away from the bustling international seaport of Salem Town. The two populations argued over taxes, the location of the shared meetinghouse and whether Salem Town's focus on international shipping was morally dubious. In the two decades before the witch outbreak, Salem Village was granted a small measure of autonomy by the colonial government to build its own meetinghouse and hire a minister who reflected the community's values. This new independence also left the Village in a legal limbo, with no civic administration or clear bureaucratic structure.

In 1684 the Massachusetts Bay Colony, which included Salem Village, lost its charter (which gave the colony legal rights and protections). It had been stripped because of repeated violations, particularly pertaining to the prohibition on passing religious laws. And while a new charter was instated in 1691, it was more anti-religious than the first. The Puritans, who had left England because of religious persecution, feared that their way of life, what some historians have labeled an "American theocracy," was under attack. There was a sense of political instability and a threat to their autonomy and values as a Puritan colony. Meanwhile, the northeastern winters were harsh. In particular, there had been a recent outbreak of smallpox and an increase of raids by Native tribes. The colony's unresolved legal status left the Puri-

A WITCH IS APPREHENDED
This 1883 wood engraving by Howard Pyle depicts the arrest of an accused witch—stereotypically, an older, impoverished female—in the streets of Salem Village in 1692.

tans' way of life up in the air, while at the same time they perceived that their physical bodies were under attack from enemies both seen and unseen.

Salem Village had also struggled to keep a minister. In the 16 years between 1672 and 1688, three different ministers had been hired and fired, all of whom had failed to earn widespread support of the parishioners. The citizens of Salem Village frequently fell into arguments among themselves over the merits or weaknesses of a particular minister, and in the absence of a unifying religious leader, the people of Salem Village believed that their salvation was at risk.

INTO THIS BUBBLING CAULDRON OF UNCERTAINTY stepped Samuel Parris, a Harvard dropout and failed businessman. After returning to Massachusetts, Parris began training to become a minister, presumably in search of a steady income for his wife and three children. Parris

moved to Salem Village in 1689 to serve as the fourth minister for the community, although his appointment took almost a year to finalize as a result of a disagreement over his salary. When the new minister finally joined the community, he arrived as a divisive figure in a divided town, and his actions did little to win over his doubters.

According to Puritan teachings, not every individual who attended weekly services was considered a member of the church. Membership was reserved for those individuals deemed "elect" in the eyes of God. Nonmembers were excused from the meetinghouse before Communion. Parris, uninterested in soothing the discord within Salem Village, frequently highlighted the theme of "the other" in his weekly sermons. He spoke to the elect members about the spiritual warfare taking place all around them. Those who were among the saved, including Parris and the members of the church, were to face constant battle with the damned, presumably including his many critics in Salem Village.

During the middle of January 1692, Abigail Williams and Betty Parris—the 11-year-old niece and 9-year-old daughter of Samuel Parris, respectively—fell ill. The girls were "sadly Afflicted of they knew not what Distempers," according to eyewitness Rev. John Hale, as quoted in historian Mary Beth Norton's *In the Devil's Snare*. Hale noted that the children "were bitten and pinched by invisible agents; their arms, necks, and backs turned this way and that way, and returned back again, so as it was impossible for them to do of themselves, and beyond the power of any Epileptick Fits, or natural Disease to effect."

A concerted effort to pray over the girls did little to alleviate these issues. As news of the girls' affliction spread throughout the community, so too did the symptoms. In short order, two more girls, Ann Putnam Jr., age 12, and Betty Hubbard, 17, also suffered fits. In a town with little else to do in the midst of a New England winter, the convulsions of the girls quickly became a public spectacle.

In the meantime, Samuel Parris called upon William Griggs, "the only physician in Salem Village," for advice. Using

more guesswork than doctoring, Griggs examined the girls and diagnosed that they were "under an Evil Hand." Up to this point, the situation in Salem Village, namely a small collection of children suffering from convulsions and fits, was not terribly unusual in 17th-century America. Yet an act originating in Reverend Parris's household served as a catalyst to turn a local event into a regional crisis—and was the first indication that something diabolical was afoot.

A member of Parris's congregation ordered the slaves Tituba and John Indian, a couple owned by Samuel Parris, to bake a witch cake to identify the culprit. Composed of the victims' urine mixed with rye meal and baked in the ashes of a fire, the witch cake was then fed to the Parris family dog. According to the folk tradition, the cake would reveal the source of the enchantment. Shortly thereafter the afflicted girls named Tituba herself as the source of their pain. According to Hale's eyewitness account, "The Afflicted persons cryed out of the Indian Woman . . . that she did pinch, prick, and grievously torment them, and that they saw her here and there, where no body else could."

Tituba's naming as the first witch of Salem Village fits the typical pattern in a witch hunt, as it is often an outsider who is first accused. The historical record of her biography is somewhat mixed, but she likely came into Parris's possession during his time as a businessman in the Caribbean. Contemporary accounts describe her

UNDER ENCHANTMENT
Above, Tituba, one of the first accused witches of Salem, with her accusers, Betty Parris and Abigail Williams. Opposite, Puritans sometimes attempted to deliver a woman using prayer.

as an Indian, while later historians labeled her as either half-Indian or half-African. Whatever her origin, Tituba was regarded as distinct from the white settlers of Massachusetts. As the live-in slave of the Parris house, Tituba knew the afflicted girls, despite her status as an outsider within the larger community. Historian Norton sees significance in the timing of naming Tituba a witch, as it occurred less than a month after a particularly violent Indian raid against the settlement of York and "following more than three years of unrelenting frontier warfare." Tituba represented one of the Village's great fears and embodied the outsider role of a witch.

WITHIN A COUPLE OF WEEKS, TWO OF THE GIRLS from outside the Parris household, Ann Putnam Jr. and Betty Hubbard, began to suffer from additional convulsions. Hubbard and Putnam named three witches as their tormentors: Tituba, Sarah Good and Sarah Osborne. Hubbard's testimony likely spurred the authorities to action, since at 17, her age made her eligible to testify in court in capital cases. Alongside Tituba, the two other women charged

in February 1692 with "Witchcraft, by them Committed and thereby much injury don[e]" fit the traditional profile of a witch. As in the earlier European witch hunts, the typical Salem witch was more often than not female, older and poor—and often considered quarrelsome or unpleasant.

Osborne, 49 years old when arrested, had been involved in a land dispute over her former husband's estate with her sons, who had been defended by the Putnam family. Her second husband was a young man whom she had purchased as an indentured servant, and they lived together for years before marrying. Osborne's age, the questions about her character and her place in the center of a dispute with the family of one of the bewitched girls all marked her as a likely witch.

Good, for her part, was poor woman and was considered a nuisance by her neighbors. Married to a day laborer, she begged door-to-door for relief, but the Puritans did not value pity. Economic prosperity was God's way of rewarding hard work. Poverty was a sign of sloth. Rumors of her malfeasance stretched back years, from bewitching her neighbors to killing their livestock. All three of these women faced a significant hurdle to save their lives.

The two men tasked with leading the investigation into the charges were the local magistrates, John Hathorne and Jonathan Corwin. Hathorne and Corwin were experienced justices of the peace with hundreds of investigations to their names. However, 17th-century investigations bore little resemblance to modern legal proceedings. Salem's magistrates approached the accused with a presumption of guilt and the goal of eliciting a confession. The three accused women would need to convince this skeptical pair of their innocence to have any chance of survival.

Good vehemently denied the charge of witchcraft. Witnesses were called to attest to her lack of church attendance and her propensity to mutter when leaving a house of someone who refused to offer her charity. When the magistrates pressed her on what she muttered, Good responded, "The commandments." When asked which one, she said, "If I must tell you, it is a psalm." Asked what psalm,

Good was silent, then uttered a barely audible murmur of some part of a psalm. Everyone in attendance understood this to be a sign of her guilt, since it was commonly known that witches could not recite prayers.

Osborne tried a slightly different tack and tried to claim her own affliction. She testified that she "either saw or dreamed...A thing like an Indian, all black...pinched her in her neck and pulled her by the back part of her head to the door of the house." Despite her claims, no one present believed her story, due in large part to the response of the four afflicted girls in the meetinghouse. Every time Good or Osborne spoke, the girls would yell and writhe about the place. The fact that the sound of the accused women's voices caused such anguish was interpreted by all as a sign of their guilt.

Tituba's examination took a different turn altogether. Rather than denying the charge of witchcraft, she immediately offered a full confession. Some historians have speculated that Samuel Parris beat a full confession out of his slave prior to her examination. The theory makes a good deal of sense. The presence of witchcraft within the minister's own home was likely a cause of acute embarrassment for Parris. A quick resolution and a full confession from the witch might help alleviate his sense of shame.

It's possible, however, that Tituba read the mood of the village. By confessing to the charges and begging for mercy, Tituba spied an opening to save her life. Whatever her motivation, Tituba spent four days electrifying the audience with tales of her bewitchment. The magistrates, wittingly or not, asked leading questions that allowed her to provide the answers that the assembled masses longed to hear. Tituba confessed that Good and Osborne told her to attack Putnam with a knife. More ominously, Tituba spoke of a "tall man" who wore all black, forced her to pinch Betty and Abigail, tempted her with pretty things and asked her to serve him for six years. The man carried a book signed by those who agreed to follow him. Under questions from the magistrates, Tituba testified that Good had signed her name to this diabolical book. When the magistrates asked how many names were in the book, Tituba answered, "Nine. Some in Boston and some herein this Towne." Intentionally or not, Tituba's testimony paved the way for the witch hunt to follow, while her confession allowed her to survive the ordeal.

On March 7, 1692, Good, Osborne and Tituba were sent to a Boston jail to await their formal trial. Two months

HERE LIES GRANNY
Opposite, an engraving of Sarah "Granny" Good, who was actually pregnant when accused and lost her infant in jail before being hanged. Above, a sign marking the home of Rev. Samuel Parris.

later, the witch hunt would claim its first victim when Osborne died in custody. While most villagers felt some relief at finding the three witches, Tituba's warning of the "tall man" and the nine names in his book continued to stoke the fears of the community.

BACK IN SALEM VILLAGE, NOT EVERYONE WAS convinced by the testimony of the four girls. A woman named Martha Corey laughed when told of the behavior of the girls and their supposed demonic possession. Unfortunately for Corey, the Puritan rumor mill began to churn, and word spread of her skepticism. Although an elected church member, Corey was described as outspoken and opinionated, dangerous traits for a woman to have in the midst of a witch hunt. Several times between March 7 and 12, the 12-year-old Ann Putnam suffered a bout of shakes and tremors. When asked whom she saw torturing her, Putnam named Corey.

COREY MAINTAINED HER INNOCENCE UNDER questioning and cast doubt on the girls accusing people of witchcraft: "Nay, we must not believe distracted persons." Despite her denials, the girls sat in the audience shrieking in pain every time Corey moved. One of the girls cried out that there was a "black man" whispering into Corey's ear, while others swore that a host of witch-es were gathered on the lawn outside the meetinghouse. Even Corey's husband testified against her, claiming that he found it difficult to pray in her presence. At one point, Martha Corey said, "You can't prove me a witch." Unfortunately

for her, she could not prove she was not one, and she was sent to jail, first in Salem, and then in Boston, in March 1692.

The pace of the witch hunt increased again as fear gripped the region over concerns of the mysterious black man (presumably the same devil figure Tituba had described, but the "afflicted" girls accused a black man instead of a tall and white one) and his growing legion of witches. Good's 4- or 5-year-old daughter, Dorcas, was arrested and sent to the prison in Boston. Although the child was too young to hang, the authorities believed claims from Ann Putnam Jr. and one other that her specter had bit and pinched them in their homes. Dorcas ultimately survived the more than seven months she spent chained in prison, though the arrest of a child so young demonstrates the level of hysteria and fear present in and around Salem.

The next person to be accused was

CASE CLOSED
Martha Corey argued with prosecutors in 1692. Her husband, Giles Corey, testified against her, but he was also accused of witchcraft. She was hanged, and he was crushed to death.

a surprise to the people of Salem Village: Rebecca Nurse, an elderly but pious and widely admired woman who had raised eight children. She was the wife of Francis Nurse, an artisan who rose in status and eventually purchased a 300-acre farm. The raising of the Nurse family's collective station through landownership was met with resentment and border disputes by some neighbors, notably the Putnams. As the Salem Village rumor mill began to churn, a couple of people recalled Nurse growing angry at a neighbor for the destruction of her garden by the neighbor's hogs shortly before that neighbor died.

In short order, both Ann Putnam Jr. and her mother named Rebecca Nurse as the specter responsible for their recent torment. At her examination, Nurse consistently denied the charges and, in typical Puritan steadfastness, accepted her fate as the will of God. Nurse was sent to the Salem Town prison, but the rest of Salem Village remained on edge. Rev. Deodat Lawson, one of Salem's previous ministers, was quoted by historian John Demos as describing the mood thusly, "The whole assembly was struck with consternation, and they were afraid that those that sat next to them were under the influence of witchcraft."

The month of April saw 21 people arrested for questioning by the magistrates. Among this latest batch of accused were several who fit the traditional profile of a witch, including Bridget Bishop, an unpopular older woman who had previously been accused of witchcraft, and Abigail Hobbs, an irreverent 14-year-old who had been known for saying she had "sold her selfe boddy & Soull to the old boy," and was frequently seen wandering the woods at night. The arrest of five men accused of witchcraft during the month was the first instance of accusations crossing the gender line in Salem. Although not unique in the longer history of witch hunts, the charges against these men signaled a deepening crisis. Yet it was Ann Putnam Jr.'s report of seeing the "apparition of a minister" who "tore me all to pieces," along with the subsequent confession of the recently arrested Deliverance Hobbs, that took Salem into its next darker phase.

George Burroughs served as the minister of Salem from 1680 to 1683, an unhappy tenure marked by numerous arguments with some of his parishioners. After resigning the pulpit, Burroughs was arrested for unpaid debts owed to the Putnam family. Burroughs fought the charge, produced witnesses to vouch for his financial honesty and was ultimately exonerated of the charge. John Putnam, husband to Ann, was publicly humiliated in front of his peers. It's not a far leap to speculate that this episode

Good's 4- or 5-year-old daughter, Dorcas, was arrested and sent to the prison in Boston. The child was too young to hang.

— △ —

played a role in Ann Putnam Jr.'s naming of Burroughs as the spectral minister.

During the examination of Burroughs, a multitude of former parishioners testified to the magistrates about his unnatural and likely diabolical strength. Stories were told of Burroughs lifting a "very heavy gun . . . at arm's length with only [a] finger" and moving full casks of cider easily. However, the main charge leveled against Burroughs was "spectral murder." One of the afflicted girls testified that ghosts of his dead wives appeared in the meetinghouse and accused Burroughs of murdering them. When Deliverance Hobbs, who had confessed to witchcraft after her April 23 arrest, accused Burroughs of preaching to "a meeting [of witches] . . . and pressed them to bewitch all in the Village," the former minister's fate was sealed.

WHEN BOTH ABIGAIL AND DELIVERANCE HOBBS'S confessions were made public, fear and belief in the devil's work gripped the region. The core group of girls who made the accusations took full advantage of the hysteria. As spring turned to summer, the pace of accusations and spectral sightings accelerated. By the end of April, 29 individuals stood accused of witchcraft. Two months later, the total was 68. Not only were the number of sightings and accusations increasing, but witches and apparitions also began to appear beyond the borders of Salem Village and Salem Town. Amesbury, some 40 miles north of Salem Village, witnessed its first accusation by May 1. As the fear continued to spread, the colonial government in Boston realized that this localized affair showed no sign of stopping and finally intervened.

In May, Sir William Phips, recently appointed governor of Massachusetts, arrived to bring order to a colony in crisis. Phips oversaw the creation of a legal structure meant to deal with the growing number of witch-related cases. Rather than free the women and men being held in prison, Phips created the Court of Oyer and Terminer ("to hear and determine"), led by Lieutenant Governor William Stoughton, to serve as judges for the witch trials and lend authority and legitimacy to the accusations.

The first trial took place on June 2. Bridget Bishop stood

The court would use the "touch test": the presence of the accused would, for instance, cause the assembled girls to scream and writhe in pain.

— △ —

as defendant, although the commission decided to treat the preliminary examination by the magistrates as sufficient. In addition to the "afflicted" girls thrashing throughout her testimony, 10 villagers had relayed tales of misfortunes—being tormented by black pigs and flying monkeys, bewitched and dead children and women, a poppet (voodoo doll) found in Bishop's basement—that occurred after arguments with Bishop. Finally, a humiliating body examination revealed that she had a witches' mark in her genital area. There was no attempt to litigate the charges anew. The decision to try the 60-year-old woman first demonstrated the prosecution's belief that the accusations and proof against her were ironclad. And on June 10, 1692, Bishop became the first Salem witch to be hanged.

The court did not meet again until the end of the month. During this hiatus, a swell of opposition to the proceedings surfaced. One of the magistrates, Nathaniel Saltonstall, resigned in protest. A petition circulated, and a campaign to save Rebecca Nurse and challenge the veracity of the afflicted girls was gaining support. Then Governor Phips asked the colony's clergy for a theological assessment of the court's procedures. At issue was how the court interpreted the testimony of the collection of girls. By and large, their accusations were founded on spectral evidence. One girl claimed she saw an apparition of an individual typically involved in some malicious act, although no one else present could see such an apparition. Such "spectral evidence" had to this point been deemed sufficient to render a guilty verdict by the local magistrates. The court's use of the "touch test" was also in question. The presence of the accused would, for instance, cause the assembled girls to scream and writhe in pain. The magistrates would force the accused to literally touch the skin of one of the suffering girls. If the touch quieted the girl, then the accused was deemed guilty of witchcraft.

Given an opportunity to shed a little rationality on the proceedings, the ministers hedged. In a carefully worded letter penned by Cotton Mather (one of the ministers), they warned against the use of spectral evidence and the touch test, stating that innocents could be implicated. At the same time, they praised the commission and urged it to

render a "speedy and vigorous prosecution of such as have rendered themselves obnoxious." Armed with this conflicting advice, the Court of Oyer and Terminer chose the path of "speedy and vigorous prosecution" of the accused. The witch crisis was spreading. Two of the original afflicted girls—records suggest that they were Mercy Lewis, 19, and Betty Hubbard, 17—traveled to nearby Andover, 12 miles away, to help a man named Joseph Ballard detect if his ailing wife was bewitched. The girls were quickly gaining a reputation as skilled witch finders, and once there, they put their talents to good use in other homes. Their witch finding kicked off a wave of accusations that led to more than 40 formal witchcraft accusations in Andover between July and September.

AT DEATH'S DOOR
Above, Bridget Bishop, the first woman executed on charges of witchcraft; opposite, Rev. George Burroughs. Both were tried and convicted of witchcraft, then hanged to death.

Meanwhile, back in Salem Village, during the first week of August, the next court session took place, featuring the trials of six individuals. Once again, the proceedings were largely ceremonial and ended with two women and four men, including former minister Burroughs, sentenced to death by hanging.

On the day of the execution, Burroughs began to recite the Lord's Prayer as he stepped onto the scaffolding. The gathered crowd was moved to tears, and there was a collective murmur of fear that this was a sign of Burroughs's innocence. But Mather spoke up at that moment, reminding the crowd that Burroughs was "no ordained minister" and pointing out that "the devil has often been transformed into an angel of light."

Fifteen more convictions in September were handed down, and nine executions were carried out. One of the accused, Giles Corey, simply refused to answer the charges against him, choosing in the legal parlance to "stand mute." In response, the court ordered Corey to undergo *peine forte et dure* ("strong and hard punishment"), wherein heavy stones were placed on his chest and gradually increased to compel his testimony. Corey was tortured for three days and is reported to have said only, "More weight," before being crushed to death.

THROUGHOUT THE SALEM WITCH HUNT, THERE were concessional signs that the girls' accusations were not always accepted wholeheartedly. In a notable exchange during the trial of Rebecca Nurse, one of the affected girls shouted out the name of Samuel Willard and accused him of afflicting her with wizardry. Willard, who served as the pastor of the Old South Street Church in Boston, was a pillar of the Puritan community. Upon hearing Willard's name, one of the magistrates told her firmly, "No, you must be mistaken," and had her sent out of the court. The ignored accusation indicates that at least a portion of the blame for the tragedy of Salem lies squarely on the shoulders of the judges and legal authorities of the Massachusetts colony who failed to put an end to the spiraling accusations.

Eventually, however too late, the legal and moral authorities of the colony began to reassert themselves and put an end to the witch hunt during the fall of 1692. The execution of Burroughs, "a scripture-spouting minister, protesting his innocence," in the words of historian Stacy Schiff, seemed to mark a turning point. A number of the judges involved with the trials began to express doubts about the process.

Unlike his son Cotton, Increase Mather worried that innocent blood had been spilled, and in early October he released *Cases of Conscience*. The book argued that proof of witchcraft required a "free and voluntary confession" and that if the court did not accept the testimony of a possessed person in a murder trial,

then "neither may we do it in the case of witchcraft." While Cotton Mather's writings that fall stand as a defense of the witch trials, his father wrote, "It is better that 10 suspected witches should escape than one innocent person should be condemned."

By the end of October, Governor Phips had dissolved the Commission of Oyer and Terminer and released most of the prisoners still in custody awaiting trial solely on the basis of spectral evidence. In December, a new Superior Court was established to hold the remainder of the trials, as Phips later reported that the former proceedings were "too violent and not grounded upon a right foundation." By May 1693, everyone accused of witchcraft was either released from jail or pardoned by the governor directly.

The fever, if not the Puritans' belief in witches, had finally broken. ▲

THE SMOKE CLEARS

IN THE AFTERMATH

The final tally of the Salem witch trials is astounding. In addition to 24 innocent people losing their lives, at least 140 were falsely imprisoned, and countless others faced debilitating rumors

By Matthew Plunkett

Once someone was accused of witchcraft, even after the shadow lifted, it often meant disaster. Those eventually freed from prison faced extreme economic suffering as a result of the accusations. Many had been absent from their homes for months. For example, Philip English ran a highly successful import business before he and his wife fled the region to escape a charge of witchcraft. When they returned, the Englishes found their warehouses emptied and looted; their home had been ransacked, with "family portraits, wines, clothing, five pigs" among the missing items.

Others, sent to prison, received staggering bills. In the 17th century, prisons charged prisoners for food and shelter, even if the charges were later dropped. For many living hand-to-mouth, such debts could prove crippling, especially because under Massachusetts law, prisoners were not to be released from jail until their fines were paid. One victim of this debtors' system was Lydia Dustin, who died in prison in March 1693 despite being acquitted the month before.

One of the more brazen acts of the entire episode, as historian Mary Beth Norton highlights in her book,

occurred in the fall of 1692 as the Massachusetts legislature rushed to create a new judicial system for the colony. Among other provisions, the legislature passed a new anti-witchcraft law that included one significant alteration. Previously, the law held that the property and goods of a hanged witch were to be preserved for the heirs of the guilty party. During the witch crisis in Salem, the sheriff of Essex County, George Corwin, seized all or part of several estates belonging to some of the hanged witches. Historians generally agree that the revised Massachusetts law was designed to protect Corwin's ill-gotten gains. Even after their death, the system remained tilted unfairly against the accused of Salem.

As the calendar turned to 1693, the people of Salem Village and the surrounding towns were left to pick up the pieces and attempt to mend relationships with their fellow townspeople. The witch trials had sown "division and a sore sickness of spirit on the people," tearing apart families. Once-friendly neighbors had accused one another of witchcraft and malice. When the collective fever finally broke, those who remained were left with anger, resentment and guilt. The process of healing

THE WITCH JAIL
Some trial victims were forced to remain in prison even after they were exonerated. This cellar, photographed in 1949, is said to contain beams from the original jail it replaced in 1763.

would eventually take generations, but in the immediate aftermath, Salem Village began taking crucial steps.

The entire village struggled economically in the aftermath of the witch trials, which had pulled farmers from their fields when the planting needed to be done. But more important, there was a growing recognition of Samuel Parris's culpability in the trials. In a final attempt to hold on to his lucrative post, Parris delivered a sermon from the pulpit titled "Meditations for Peace," wherein he acknowledged that the devil might "take the shape of the innocent" and that relying solely on the testimony of the afflicted might not yield the truth.

Though it was short of an apology, Parris did extend his sorrow for those impacted "through the clouds of human weakness and Satan's wiles and sophistry." Parris concluded his sermon by requesting that everyone in Salem

Village "forgive each other heartily."

Parris's words came far too late for his parishioners, particularly the Nurse family and other families of the executed. They undertook a years-long process to remove him from the office. Parris refused to quit and wanted what he believed was his due payment, while an increasing number of churchgoers simply wished for him to leave. The argument went to court and arbitration before the two sides reached an agreement. By the summer of 1697, Parris, as well as his daughter, Betty, were forced to leave Salem Village for good.

Five years after the trials began, the Massachusetts General Court ordered "a day of prayer, with fasting" to seek God's forgiveness. Though a cynic might ask how such a minor event might benefit either those murdered by the colony or their descendants, official pronouncements along these lines were a first step toward acknowledging the errors and crimes committed during 1692. On that day, Samuel Sewall, one of the judges appointed to the Court of Oyer and Terminer, stood before his congregation of the Old South Church in Boston to offer his own message of apology, read aloud by Rev. Samuel Willard. His statement read in part, "Samuel Sewall, sensible of the reiterated strokes of God upon himself and family; and being sensible, that as to the Guilt contracted upon the opening of the late Commission of Oyer and Terminer at Salem . . . he is, upon many accounts, more concerned than any that he knows of, Desires to take the Blame and shame of it, Asking pardon of men, And especially desiring prayers that God, who has an Unlimited Authority, would pardon that sin and all other his sins."

In the decades that followed, individuals and the colonial government took steps to reckon with the tragedy of Salem. In 1709, Ann Putnam Jr. sought official membership in the Salem church. As part of her application, Putnam confessed to her role in spilling "innocent blood" and directly apologized to the family of Rebecca Nurse. One year later, the

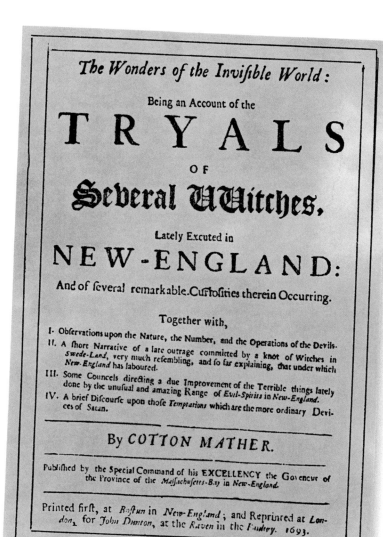

The Wonders of the Invisible World:

Being an Account of the

TRYALS

OF

Several Witches,

Lately Executed in

NEW-ENGLAND:

And of several remarkable Curiosities therein Occurring.

Together with,

I. Observations upon the Nature, the Number, and the Operations of the Devils.
II. A short Narrative of a late outrage committed by a knot of Witches in *Swede-Land*, very much resembling, and so far explaining, that under which *New-England* has laboured.
III. Some Councels directing a due Improvement of the Terrible things lately done by the unusual and amazing Range of Evil-Spirits in *New-England*.
IV. A brief Discourse upon those *Temptations* which are the more ordinary Devices of Satan.

By COTTON MATHER.

Published by the Special Command of his EXCELLENCY the Governeur of the Province of the *Massachusetts-Bay* in *New-England.*

Printed first, at *Boston* in *New-England*; and Reprinted at *London*, for *John Dunton*, at the *Raven* in the *Poultry*. 1693.

General Court allocated financial reparations for the families involved in the trials. Despite the impossibility of making amends for the lives taken, the proactive measures stand in stark contrast to the more passive reactions from governments involved in similar tragedies of future generations.

IN SEPTEMBER 1692, COTTON MATHER, THE SAME man who wrote *Memorable Providences Relating to Witchcraft and Possessions*, took the first pass at framing the events of 1692 in his book *The Wonders of the Invisible World*. The Puritan society lacked any newspapers or periodicals, and thus Mather was able to take great editorial license with his writing. Focusing on five specific trials to serve as representative of the

GRAVE MISTAKES
Opposite top, the headstone of Giles Corey, who was crushed to death after refusing to confess. Opposite below, the headstone of judge John Hathorne. Above, Cotton Mather's 1693 pamphlet on the witchcraft delusions.

SECRET BURIAL
This monument in the Nurse family burial ground in modern-day Salem Village, now Danvers, carries a tribute to Rebecca Nurse. Her family secretly rescued her body from Proctor's Ledge shortly after her hanging and likely transported it here.

> External pressures from enemies and the environment, combined with the interfamilial feuds common in small towns, all played a role in forming the crisis.

— △ —

whole, Mather deliberately ignored and/or failed to report many of the more embarrassing and legally dubious actions taken during these proceedings, including the original innocent verdict in the trial of Rebecca Nurse.

Mather was far from the last to try to explain what happened in Salem. For the next 300 years, dozens of historians, psychologists and scientists, including John Demos in his 2008 book, *The Enemy Within: 2,000 Years of Witch-Hunting in the Western World*, have examined the events of 1692 and offered explanations about how the tragedy occurred.

In the immediate aftermath of Salem, the prevailing reason accorded the events was divine retribution. The belief in witchcraft and the devil remained fixed, so the events were viewed through the lens of good versus evil. The events of Salem were a form of God's punishment for the collective sin of the people of Salem Village.

The debate around Salem has engrossed many. Some cast blame on Tituba and her husband for "the wild and strange superstitions prevalent among their native tribes." One author cited the possibility of ergot poisoning and its ability to cause hallucinations and violent muscle spasms. Others have pointed to the unique worldview of the Puritans and the threat of violence posed by Native American attacks.

When searching for an explanation for events such as Salem, an "all of the above" mentality usually works, although the ergot poisoning seems a stretch. Demos writes, "Witch-hunts, like most large social and historical phenomena, invariably show a pattern of multiple causation." External pressures from enemies and the environment, combined with the interfamilial feuds common in small towns and the social and religious pressures placed on adolescent females, all played a role in forming the crisis.

For a modern audience, these factors may seem a relic of an earlier time. However, the threat of mass hysteria and mass violence remains. One need only examine the history of the 20th century to realize that these dangers still persist today. ▲

Witchcraft Act of 1735

The British Parliament passed an act reversing the laws that were on the books

—

With the simple passing of a law, the legal mandate for the hunting and execution of witches in the Kingdom of Great Britain and its colonies came to a conclusion. The law, which reversed the Scottish Witchcraft Act of 1563 and the English Witchcraft Act of 1604, made it a crime to claim that any person was guilty of practicing witchcraft or had supernatural powers. Culprits found guilty and given the maximum penalty simply found themselves imprisoned for a year. Yet the new law was not without imperfections. Intended to prosecute persons for fraud rather than for cavorting with the devil, the 1735 Act was often used against spiritualists and, in particular, the transient Romani population. In 1951, the law was replaced by the Fraudulent Mediums Act, which prohibited persons from claiming to be a psychic, medium or any sort of spiritualist with intent to deceive and make money from that deception. Eventually replaced by consumer-protection regulations that prohibit any service that can't deliver on its promise, the 1735 Act is still in force in several countries: Northern Ireland (where it has never been invoked), Israel (where it applies only to for-profit practitioners) and South Africa (where the Witchcraft Suppression Act of 1957 is based on similar legislation).

Time and progress erased many of the infamous Salem witch trials' original buildings, but Salem still features plenty of eerie sites where inquisitive visitors can connect with the city's dark history. In 1945 and 1949, photographers Jerry Cooke and Nina Leen visited Salem to take photos of key locations, several of which appeared in *Life* magazine

By Nancy Lambert

HIDDEN PAST

Accused witches imprisoned at Salem Gaol suffered torture and endured horrid living conditions while awaiting their fates, some dying before they even saw trial. Abandoned in 1813, the Old Witch Jail and Dungeon was eventually sold and converted into the home pictured here. Though later owners featured exhibitions of artifacts and hosted historically themed tours, Salem never formally preserved the site, eventually razing it to make way for a new building in 1956. But during construction, workers discovered the Witch Dungeon beneath the home and recovered original beams, now displayed at local museums and exhibits.

Salem
1692

PAYING FOR TIME

In 1862, Salem erected the Essex County Superior Court building, seen above, just around the corner from where the original Salem courthouse stood until 1760. Now, only a weathered plaque on the Masonic Temple notes the place where most of Salem's accused witches faced trial. Right: The accused paid for their time in prison, literally, as evidenced by this jailer's bill for several people held at Salem Gaol in 1693. The bills—due even in the event of a prisoner's acquittal or death—included charges for the shackles, irons and locks used to restrain them.

JAILER'S BILL FOR BOARD OF THE WITCHES

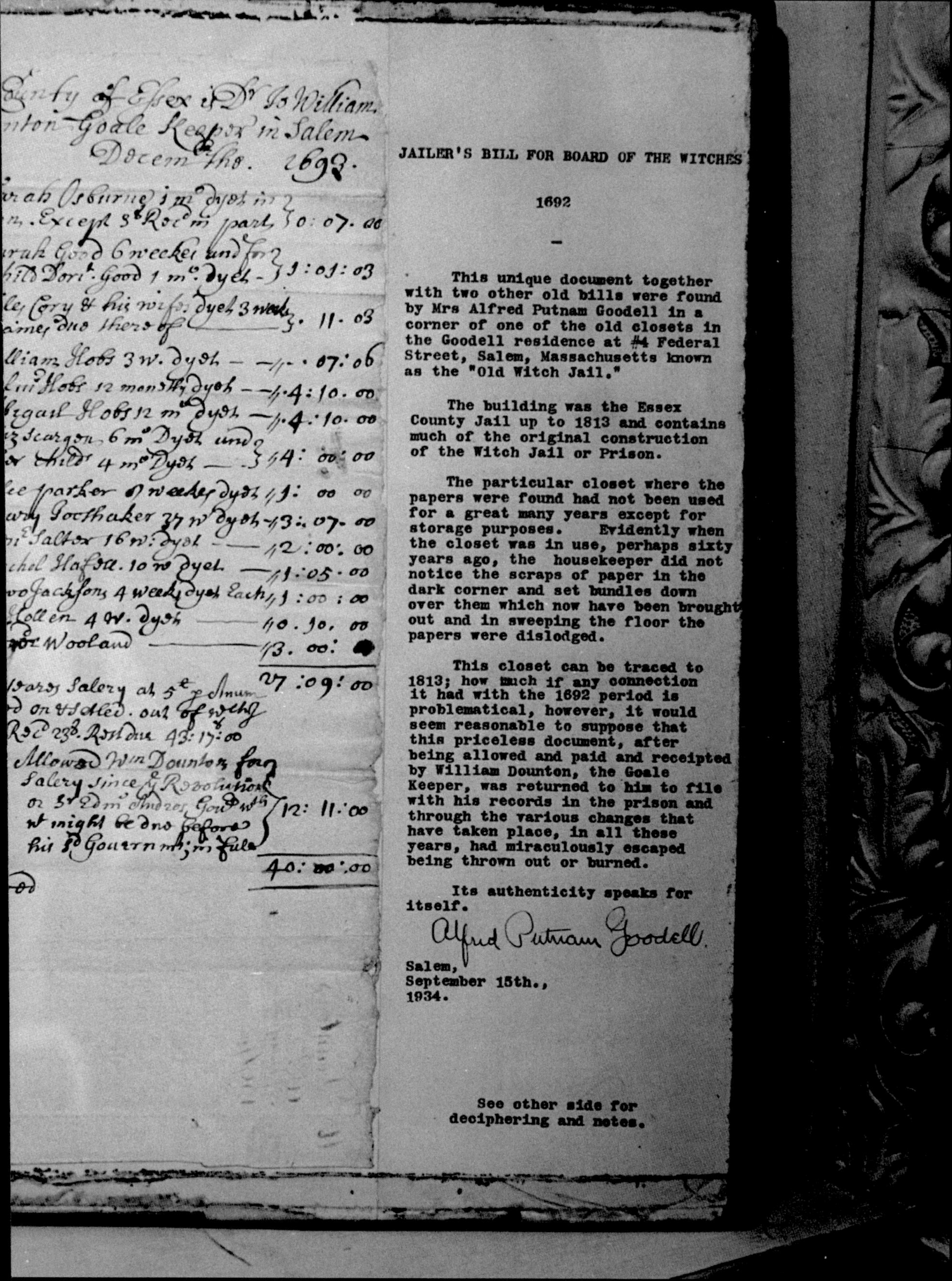

1692

-

This unique document together with two other old bills were found by Mrs Alfred Putnam Goodell in a corner of one of the old closets in the Goodell residence at #4 Federal Street, Salem, Massachusetts known as the "Old Witch Jail."

The building was the Essex County Jail up to 1813 and contains much of the original construction of the Witch Jail or Prison.

The particular closet where the papers were found had not been used for a great many years except for storage purposes. Evidently when the closet was in use, perhaps sixty years ago, the housekeeper did not notice the scraps of paper in the dark corner and set bundles down over them which now have been brought out and in sweeping the floor the papers were dislodged.

This closet can be traced to 1813; how much if any connection it had with the 1692 period is problematical, however, it would seem reasonable to suppose that this priceless document, after being allowed and paid and receipted by William Dounton, the Goale Keeper, was returned to him to file with his records in the prison and through the various changes that have taken place, in all these years, had miraculously escaped being thrown out or burned.

Its authenticity speaks for itself.

Alfred Putnam Goodell

Salem,
September 15th.,
1934.

See other side for deciphering and notes.

PINNING DOWN THE TRUTH

Gallows Hill, long rumored to be the spot where
19 victims of the trials were hanged for witchcraft,
is just above the actual location of the executions, a
rocky crevice that a team of experts recently identified
as Proctor's Ledge. Soon after, Salem built and dedicated a memorial on the site for the victims. Right: The
home of Rebecca Nurse. On the following pages, the
interior of this historic home.

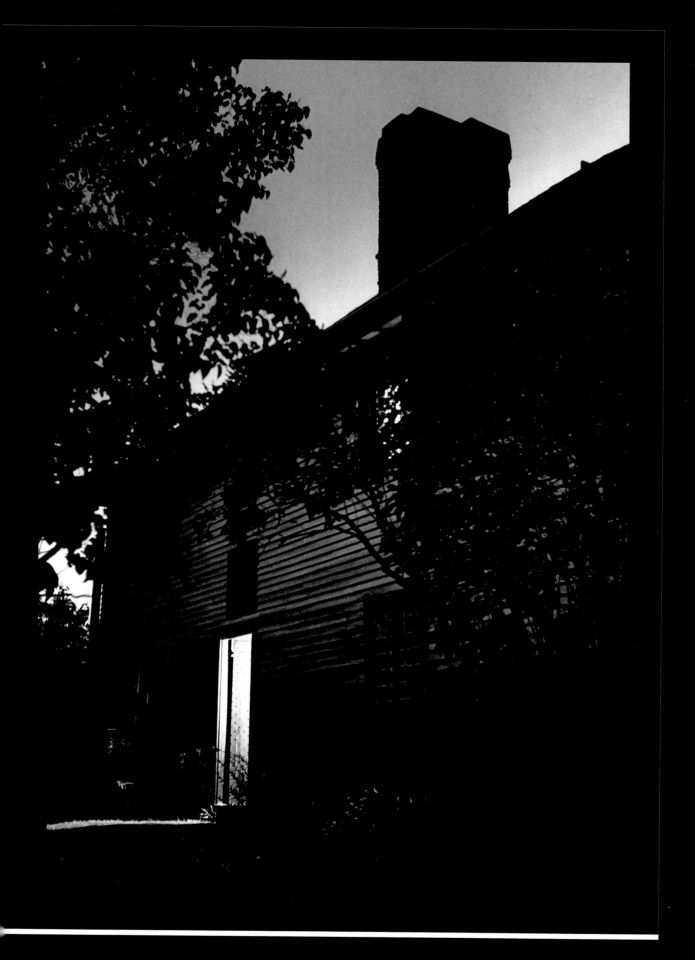

THE LONG WAY HOME
The Rebecca Nurse Homestead is the only residence of a Salem witch trials victim open to the public. Nurse was well respected, and her arrest at age 71 elicited outrage, spurring dozens of neighbors to sign a petition in her defense. Despite community outcry, a judge used the grandmother's partial deafness to flip an initial not-guilty verdict, and Nurse was hanged on July 19, 1692. After the execution, Nurse's family smuggled her remains home for burial on the property. The Homestead also houses the remains of fellow trials casualty (and father-in-law of a Nurse petitioner) George Jacobs Sr.

BONFIRE GATHERING
Celebrants at the Walpurgis fire in Erfurt, Germany, dress as costumed devils and witches. The night is named for Saint Walpurga, the patron saint for the protection against witchcraft.

Modern Witchcraft

An investigation into today's Wiccan practitioners and
the depiction of witches on television and film—including
the iconic Arthur Miller play *The Crucible*

SEARCHING FOR THE OTHER

CONTEMPORARY WITCH HUNTS

The meaning of the term "witch hunt" has evolved to fit the modern
age, now understood to be shorthand for a misguided and unjustified
search for perpetrators of some wrong against society

By Matthew Plunkett

One of the first uses of "witch hunt" in the modern era occurred in July 1917. The British statesman Lord George Curzon, under fire from the British press to investigate a failed campaign in Mesopotamia during World War I, declared, "The Press has been developed on the lines of the witch hunt of barbarous African tribes." Within a year, the phrase leapfrogged across the Atlantic and entered the lexicon. In July 1918, the *Buffalo Morning Express* ran a story urging its readers to avoid taking part in a witch hunt: "The fact that you have quarreled with your neighbor is not a good enough reason for reporting him to the newspapers or the Federal authorities as a German spy or a disloyal person."

After the war, the phrase continued to live primarily in the world of politics and labor. But the most famous metaphorical witch hunt in American history began in the immediate aftermath of World War II. During the war, the U.S. placed its long distrust of Communism on hold while allying with Joseph Stalin's USSR in the fight against Nazi Germany. As President Franklin Delano Roosevelt famously said, "It is permitted in time of grave danger to walk with the devil until

THE RED SCARE
Senator Joseph McCarthy
swore in author Dashiell
Hammett, known for creating
the detective Sam Spade, at the
Senate Permanent Investigating
Committee hearing in 1953.

you have crossed the bridge." After Republicans made sweeping gains in the 1946 midterm elections, the focus of Congress turned once again to the internal and external threat from Communists.

Enter Senator Joseph R. McCarthy. In February 1950, McCarthy, a first-term Republican senator from Wisconsin, took the stage in Wheeling, W. Va., and delivered a speech ostensibly focused on the birth of Abraham Lincoln. Instead, that speech called out what he believed to be the biggest threat to the safety of the U.S.—not the armed forces of the Soviet Union but traitors ensconced within the State Department. In a moment designed to heighten the drama, McCarthy brandished a sheet of paper and stated, "I have here in my hand a list of 205 . . . names that were made known to the Secretary of State as being members of the Communist Party and who nevertheless are still working and shaping policy in the State Department." While the specific number of Communists remained a moving target for McCarthy (the number shifted between 57 and 205 with regularity), McCarthy remained the symbolic head of the nation's quest to exorcise its Communist demons for the next four years, building his short-

lived career on the backs of the second Red Scare. His hunt for Communist witches spread beyond the employees in the State Department and continued into investigations of numerous government departments, academics, the media and party politicians, among others.

Although McCarthy's name became synonymous with the hunt for Communist infiltrators, the witch hunt preceded and extended beyond his limited career. The fear was bipartisan. Democrats, including President Harry S. Truman, created loyalty programs to find and remove "subversives" within the federal government. As the worldwide threat of Communism increased, including control of Eastern Europe and Asia, the Soviet Union's development of the atomic bomb, the war in Korea and several high-profile espionage cases within the U.S., the anti-Communist movement gained credibility. Federal, state and local officials combed through their ranks to remove anyone associated with the Communist Party. More than 2,000 government employees lost their jobs during the Truman and Eisenhower administrations for perceived security risks. Hundreds of secondary teachers

and university professors lost their jobs or were forced to sign loyalty pledges. Famously, the Hollywood blacklist spread to include hundreds of writers, actors, producers and directors.

Millions of people throughout the country remained silent in the face of this suppression of free speech rather than risk losing their jobs, and one historian conservatively estimates the loss of jobs at 10,000. This economic fear stifled debate and fueled the actions of the anti-Communist forces. Although McCarthy's career effectively came to an end during the disastrous Army-McCarthy hearings in 1954, the specter of McCarthyism remained active in the body politic until the end of the decade.

When playwright Arthur Miller, who had penned the groundbreaking *Death of a Salesman* in 1949, watched peers testify before the House Un-American Activities Committee, he looked for an allegory for the paranoia then gripping his country. He found it in the Salem witch trials, and from this seed Miller created *The Crucible* as a metaphor not only for McCarthyism but for the way a community could destroy itself from the inside out. ▲

HOLLYWOOD ON TRIAL
Arthur Miller, with pipe, testifies before the committee. He claimed to have supported Communist causes in the late 1940s because "it suited the mood I was in." Opposite, Army legal counsel Joseph Welch, seated, listens to McCarthy during the televised hearings.

ARTHUR MILLER

THE CRUCIBLE

Arthur Miller's classic channeled the Salem
witch trials and cast a light on the manipulation of the fear
of Communism in mid-century America

By Daniel S. Levy

I n the spring of 1952, Arthur Miller spent a week in Salem, Mass. While there, he paged through documents from the 1692 witch trials, stopped at the local museum to examine pins that children had claimed the devil had used to jab their flesh and visited what was then thought to be the spot where hanging gibbets once loomed.

At the time, America was grappling with a Red Scare set off by Senator Joseph McCarthy's assertion that Communists had ensconced themselves throughout society. Miller felt that the events in Salem could allow him to explore the eerie parallels between 17th-century Massachusetts and postwar America. "McCarthy's power to stir fears of creeping Communism was not entirely based on illusion, of course," Miller wrote in *The New Yorker* in 1996. "The paranoid, real or pretended, always secretes its pearls around a grain of fact."

As the Tony Award–winning author of *Death of a Salesman* searched for a clue to the truth, he found a report by Samuel Parris. The minister wrote how during the trial, his niece, Abigail Williams, lightly touched Elizabeth Proctor and "immediately Abigail cried out,

her fingers, her fingers, burned." For Miller, this passage birthed the germ of an idea for *The Crucible*. "In this remarkably observed gesture of a troubled young girl, I believed, a play became possible . . . By this time, I was sure, John Proctor had bedded Abigail . . . That Abigail started, in effect, to condemn Elizabeth to death with her touch . . . was quite suddenly the human center of all this turmoil."

Miller's play closely follows the actual occurrences in that town of giddy young girls "dancing like heathen in the forest," the spiraling accusations of "hurtful, vengeful spirits layin' hands on these children" and the death of infants. And while there is no evidence that the 11-year-old Williams knew the Proctors or why she made her claim, Miller created a relationship to not only propel her charge but also use Proctor's guilt and struggle to transform him into "the most forthright voice against the madness around him." And with the play's lethal brew of the supernatural, illicit sexuality and what Rev. John Hale decried as "the vengeance of a little girl," Miller crafted the perfect metaphor for McCarthyism.

The author's biographer Christopher Bigsby observed in the TV documentary *None Without Sin* how for

SALEM "WITCH PINS"
During the trials, witnesses testified that witches used straight pins like these to torment their victims, sometimes appearing in court with pins dramatically stuck in their necks and arms.

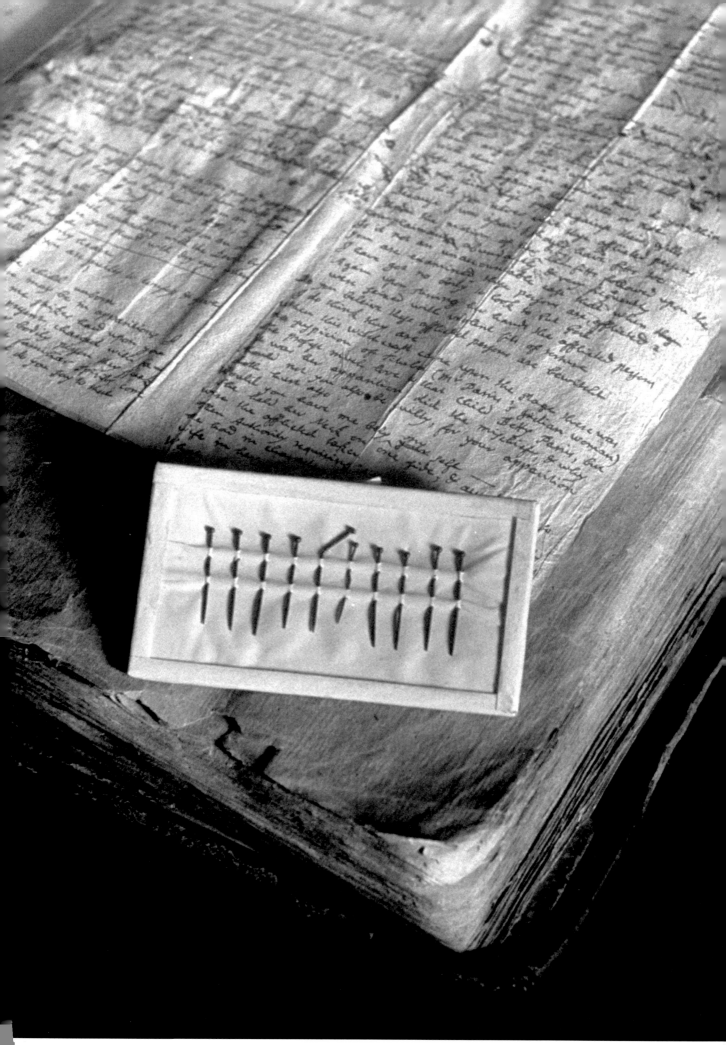

Miller writing *The Crucible* became "an urgent piece of political and social commitment." So many practices he learned of in Salem mirrored the probes used by both Mc-Carthy in the Senate and the House Un-American Activities Committee (HUAC). The dread created by the government rippled through society and allowed those claiming righteousness to judge the innocent guilty and forced Americans to turn on friends.

One of those who named names was Miller's close friend Elia Kazan. The director had staged Miller's *All My Sons* and *Death of a Salesman* on Broadway, and Miller wrote a screenplay for him that the two had tried to make in Hollywood. Both even dated Marilyn Monroe, with Miller marrying her in 1956. But on Miller's

FAME AND FORTUNE
Opposite, Miller with his wife, Marilyn Monroe, in 1956. Above, actors Madeleine Sherwood, Arthur Kennedy and Walter Hampden during a Broadway production of *The Crucible*.

way to research in Salem, he visited Kazan and learned that his friend had decided to capitulate to the HUAC. Despite an earlier refusal, Kazan fingered a number of his former theater collaborators as being fellow travelers. Miller wrote in his memoir years later that he drove away filled more with sorrow than anger. On Miller's way home from Salem, Kazan's testimony was confirmed on the radio, and the two didn't speak again for 10 years.

Miller's allegorical take on McCarthyism premiered on Broadway in January 1953. Its unquiet distillation of modern America unsettled audiences trying to grapple with current events. "It's impossible to understand how difficult those times were for everybody," recalled Madeleine Sherwood, who played Abigail

The Crucible went on to win two Tony Awards, one for best play. Meanwhile, the Red Scare continued, with Miller summoned before HUAC in 1956.

— △ —

Williams. "Very good people that just couldn't face the fact that they might lose their livelihood, their families, their dignity."

The Crucible went on to win two Tony Awards, one for best play. Meanwhile, the Red Scare continued, and Miller received a summons from HUAC in 1956. Unlike Kazan, he was not cowed. With Monroe at his side, the Pulitzer Prize winner refused to invoke his Fifth Amendment right against self-incrimination. Instead, the playwright embraced the First Amendment's guarantee of free speech, telling the representatives, "I could not use the name of another person and bring trouble on him."

Since then, *The Crucible* has become Miller's most regularly staged work. The play has sold millions of copies and has become a required read for students not much older than the preteen Williams. Eventually, it made its way to the big screen, first with a 1957 film adaptation by French existentialist philosopher Jean-Paul Sartre starring Simone Signoret and Yves Montand as the ill-fated Proctor pair.

It took a while to make its way to the U.S., partly because McCarthy's Red Scare made it an unappealing project. But in the mid-1990s, *The Crucible* was filmed with Daniel Day-Lewis and Joan Allen starring as the Proctors and Winona Ryder as Williams. Prior to the start of filming, Day-Lewis made a pilgrimage to Miller's home in Roxbury, Conn. There the three-time Academy Award winner met Miller's daughter, Rebecca, an independent filmmaker known for the 2005 *The Ballad of Jack and Rose*. They dated, saw each other on the film's Hog Island, Mass., set and married a mere two weeks before the film's November 1996 premiere.

Williams vanishes at the end of *The Crucible*, and wondering what happened to her, Roberto Aguirre-Sacasa penned a sequel play. In *Abigail/1702: A Twice Told Tale*, which premiered during the 2012 New York Stage and Film season, Chloë Sevigny portrayed Williams as she struggles to build a new life, but she's still plagued by the blood pact that she had once made. Like Williams, America continues to be haunted by both the events in Salem and McCarthyism. Miller's play stands as a powerful reminder of the abuses of power and the consequences of lies. ▲

HOLLYWOOD DEBUT
In 1996, *The Crucible* hit the big screen with Daniel Day-Lewis starring as John Proctor (center).

ANY WITCH WAY

As witches in movies and television evolved from one-dimensional stereotypes to multifaceted characters, these standout portrayals helped raise onscreen witches to new heights

By Nancy Lambert

Nothing is more terrify- ing than a powerful woman. At least, that seems to be the take-away from the earliest portrayals of witches within Western media: all evil and malicious to the bone. This negative, one-note depiction, derived from centuries of folklore, superstition and violent witch hunts fueled by religious extremism, was cemented in pop culture by Disney's long roster of wicked witches, begin-ning with Snow White's Evil Queen.

But once *The Wizard of Oz* (1939) popularized the idea of a good witch, onscreen spell casters began to open up. Stories started to push the boundaries of black-or-white witchhood with powerful but unthreaten-ing witches—like those in *I Married a Witch* and *Bewitched*. As fictional portrayals became more complex, the line between good and bad blurred more and more; in the lighthearted romp *The Witches of Eastwick*, for instance, practitioners possessed both fluctuat-ing morals and conflicting motivations.

In the late 1990s, a witch boom subverted the good-bad trope. Viewers watching the evolution of witches in real time may not have appreciated the bounty of nuanced witch characters—like *Charmed*'s Halliwell sisters and *Practical Magic*'s multigenera-tional Owens witches—all of whom had more in common with real-life Wiccans than with fairy-tale villains. Multi-layered witch characters continued on in the 21st century as staples on supernatural dramas like *The Vampire Diaries*, *True Blood* and *Supernatural*.

But there's still much territory left to explore. Historically, films and shows have largely focused on white, Western witches and ignored (or grossly misrepresented) indig-enous and non-Western witchcraft. While the up-coming, diverse reboots of *Charmed* and *Buffy* are a step in the right direction, when onscreen witches finally catch up to their real-world counter-parts, the results will be truly magical.

1. THE WIZARD OF OZ (1939)

Glinda, the Good Witch of the North, represented virtue incarnate (Gregory Maguire's *Wicked* had another take), while her sibling, the Wicked Witch of the West, possessed the worst traits of the classic witch: sneering, cruel and even prone to a cackle or two. Glinda first asked the question that would go on to paint onscreen witches for decades after: "Are you a good witch or a bad witch?"

2. BEWITCHED (1964–1972)

Samantha's magical mishaps secured a place for quirky witches in pop culture, while her sassy, wisecracking mother, Endora, paved the way for all the snarkcasting witches who were still decades off. In a television show that subverted traditional gender roles, the cultural implications of Sam's imperfect-housewife persona offered a valuable counterpoint to other female characters on TV.

3. HOCUS POCUS (1993)

In addition to generating laughs with spells gone hilariously awry, Winifred, Sarah and Mary Sanderson rode their broomsticks to new territory by giving witches room to be purely comedic figures. The anachronistic sisters' slapstick antics as they hunted children across modern Salem neutralized their terrifying qualities and sinister motives, inviting viewers to cackle with them (as well as at them).

4

4. SABRINA THE TEENAGE WITCH (1996–2003)

The first show to really explore the teen experience from a witch's point of view, Sabrina opted to hide her abilities—and her struggle to earn them—as a way to present authentic moral quandaries and real-life conflict that resonated with tween viewers.

5. THE CRAFT (1996)

Heralding an era of grittier, darker witches, the high school outsiders turned formidable practitioners of the craft discovered that their combined energies could garner dark, even deadly, consequences almost immediately. Yet they persisted in using—and eventually abusing—their gifts to right wrongs both real and imagined, until even their best intentions warped into nightmares. The cult classic attracted remake buzz in the past.

6. BUFFY THE VAMPIRE SLAYER (1996–2003)

Arguably the most affecting witch of the '90s era, Willow Rosenberg eagerly explored all facets of her craft while her girlfriend, fellow witch Tara Maclay, firmly resisted the temptation of darker magicks. As their relationship deepened, so did Willow's power. But even after she transformed into Dark Willow, a true monster, she never completely lost her humanity, which ultimately allowed her to be redeemed through the power of friendship.

7. CHARMED (1998–2006)

Popular enough to conjure up a reboot, the original Charmed Ones—sisters Prue, Piper and Phoebe Halliwell (as well as Seasons 4–8 pinch hitter Paige Matthews)—battled supernatural baddies while grappling with

all-too-human issues, like death and heartbreak, that even the strongest spells couldn't resolve. *Charmed* stressed the importance of family as a literal and figurative source of strength for the Charmed Ones, making these witches feel relatable and grounded. The reboot, which still features a trio of sisters, will appear on the CW starting Oct. 14, 2018, and has a few key differences, including a more diverse cast, a new location and different magical abilities.

8. HARRY POTTER (2001–2011)

Even the Sorting Hat struggled to categorize the Potterverse's emotionally complicated witches and wizards, who often dwelled in ethically gray spaces. That Professor Snape committed some of the franchise's darkest deeds in the name of

unfaltering loyalty (and unflagging love); that Dumbledore risked (and lost) so many lives in pursuit of victory; that Voldemort's devastating origin story humanized otherwise unfathomable evil—all prepared *Harry Potter*'s young fandom for the complexities of adulthood awaiting them.

9. AMERICAN HORROR STORY: COVEN (2013–2014)

Coven's bevy of stellar witches—a Louisiana voodoo queen, a boho necromancer, an empath, a diva, a clairvoyant, a femme fatale and…a Stevie Nicks—struck a myriad of mystical archetypes, then turned them inside out. Older witches wielded sex appeal with their power, while younger witches, blessed with outward beauty, buckled under hideous ambition and uncontrollable impulses. Rejecting basic binaries, *Coven*'s witches captured a cultural shift in the ways women could control their own narratives.

10. A DISCOVERY OF WITCHES (2018)

Diana Bishop struggles to determine where her craft fits between the demands of her nonmagical life, the strain of her family's extensive preternatural legacy and the deadly potential of her burgeoning unique abilities. More than a century after the witch's big-screen debut, *Discovery*'s lead sorceress embodies the new norm in mainstream media—a morally ambiguous, multidimensional witch prone to making dangerous mistakes. ▲

A BRAND-NEW WITCHY WORLD

MODERN WITCHCRAFT

Forget the dusty stereotypes: today's magical practitioners are vibrant and diverse, embracing a nature-centered spirituality that evolves and grows with each new generation of witches

By Nancy Lambert

In Western culture, witchcraft is no longer an aberration punishable by torture or death. Instead, we've entered an era when witches, Wiccans and other neopagans can freely practice magick—spelled with a *k* to distinguish it from the type of illusions performed by stage magicians—in a multitude of ways, as varied and unique as the millions of individuals incorporating it into their lives today.

Although often used interchangeably in media, witchcraft and Wicca are not synonymous. Witchcraft can't be defined precisely, since different cultures continue to have different practices that fall under the moniker. However, contemporary witchcraft practiced in the U.S. is more of a personalized spiritual practice, whereas Wicca is regarded as a ditheistic (although some interpret it as monotheistic, polytheistic or pantheistic, depending on the sect), globally recognized religion with nature-focused Celtic and pagan influences, falling under the umbrella of contemporary neo-paganism. The communities definitely overlap, but not all Wiccans identify as witches, nor do all witches identify as Wiccan.

Many of the first cornerstone writings about Wicca's development drew a direct line between Wicca and ancient pagan religions, but they turned out to be pseudo-historical fiction. In truth, while influenced by those traditions, Wicca is not their direct descendant and is relatively young, as far as religions go. It originated in England in the mid-20th century with Gerald Brosseau Gardner, who had been influenced by earlier successful esoteric practices, like the mid-19th-century American Spiritualist movement and Thelema, a religion involving ritualistic magick that was founded by British occultist Aleister Crowley in 1904. Wicca, as it came to be known, emphasized the divine in nature, the practice of magic and the worshipping of the Goddess as well as other deities.

Gardner, the "father of Wicca," developed his interpretation of ancient pagan witchcraft through numerous writings, and Doreen Valiente, his coven's high priestess, dubbed "the mother of modern witchcraft," penned many scriptural texts and ceremonies. She contributed to a tome of spells and rites known as the *Book of Shadows*, which laid the groundwork for the religion and contains numerous Wiccan rituals that are still practiced today.

EFFIGY AFLAME
Walpurgis Night, once a witch's Sabbath, is celebrated today in many countries. In Prague, bonfires, witch effigies, costumes and copious amounts of beer and sausages mark the event.

By the 1960s, the movement had officially taken on the name Wicca and gained traction beyond England, especially in the U.S., where it would evolve distinct branches as it surged in popularity. Despite being deep in the throes of its own "Satanic panic" at the time, the District Court of Virginia formally recognized the decidedly unchristian Wicca as a religion in 1985 (a landmark case). But while the panic—a Fundamentalist Christian-driven campaign that stigmatized, vilified and even prosecuted those suspected of esoteric or occult affiliations—cast a chill over Wiccans, it did not stop Wicca's progress.

Flush with riot grrrls, countercultural zines and girl power, the 1990s pulsed with a new youth-led boom in third-wave feminism and

TOOLS OF THE TRADE
Above, from left, items used in
Wiccan rituals: an athame, a
ritual knife used to direct energy;
a pentacle; and a crystal sphere.
Opposite, a woman walks
through coals during a rite.

Wicca, which eventually found its way into American media, with television shows such as *Charmed* and *Buffy the Vampire Slayer*, films like *The Craft* and *Practical Magic*, and young-adult novel series including *Sweep*, *The Secret Circle* and *Circle of Three* popularizing witchcraft and Wicca for the mainstream of late Gen Xers and early millennials.

At the same time (and somewhat paradoxically for a nature-based discipline), technology expanded Wicca's reach with the advent of the World Wide Web. As the internet exploded, Wiccans and witches found an innovative way to share their craft, and the many sites and communities they initiated at that time shaped and nurtured both groups' transitions into the 21st century.

BOTH MODERN WICCA AND WITCHCRAFT CELE-brate individuality, allowing seemingly boundless freedom for interpretation and practice—both cultivate a bit of a "the only rule is that there are no rules" vibe—but if not "rules," some commonalities exist within and between them. For instance, many Wiccan sects honor the Goddess (and the Horned God), though the faith's theological diversity allows for variation here too; and while Wicca does not have one presiding holy book—unlike most other major religions—most Wiccans follow the moral code set forth in the Wiccan Rede, "An it harm none, do what ye will," and create their own *Book of Shadows*, which contains the instructions for rituals and spells that they practice.

To practice those rites, Wiccans use an altar of their choosing and creation, as well as specific, symbolic ritual tools that represent the elements. These include a black-handled knife (an athame), a broom, a wand, a pentacle, a cauldron, candles, incense and a chalice. For practitioners of witchcraft, altars are completely optional but usually used and highly individual. So are their tools, which vary as much as the witches themselves, but in ad-dition to the above items, they may include crystals, candles, photographs, household staples like salt or pins, and more organic items, like feathers, soil, water and hair—whatever will best serve for focusing the witch's intention for a given spell.

When initiating a ritual, Wiccans and witches often cast a circle—a sacred space around them. Its purpose depends on the intention; sometimes to contain their energy; sometimes to protect them from negative energy or harmful forces. They close this circle to end their ceremony or rite by thanking the otherworldly powers for assistance, sometimes with a blessing.

BOTH WICCANS AND WITCHES HAVE THE OPTION of cultivating a solitary practice or joining a coven. The structure within a coven differs among sects, and within sects, between the covens themselves. In some Wiccan covens, a high priestess or high priest (or both) leads members, while other covens adopt more egalitarian structures. Even in those covens with appointed heads, the responsibilities and power assigned to those lead-

ers varies widely. Some prominent Wiccan priests, like Stewart Farrar, stressed the importance of a coven to Wiccan initiation and practice, but despite this, the majority of Wiccans today are solitary practitioners, as are most witches.

Witchcraft offers even more variants than Wicca does. Witches may (or may not) draw some of their craft's influences from Wiccan tradition, while others customize their rituals by adding Reiki, herb lore, astrology or tarot divination. Witches also look to other cultures for customs to incorporate into their craft, particularly those connected to their own heritage. For example, a witch might blend influences from indigenous witchcraft, hoodoo (an African-American folk spirituality with West African roots), brujeria (Mexican witchcraft) or Kabbalah (Jewish mysticism) into their practice, while being mindful, of course, to avoid appropriating marginalized cultures.

This sensitivity is somewhat new, but movements in both witch and Wiccan communities are now pushing for greater cultural respect, intersectional inclusiveness and diversity in their ranks. The Progressive Wicca movement, for example, eschews some of the traditions upheld by "classic" Wicca, like gendered coven roles and deities. In the witchcraft community, swelling factions of politically active, feminist-identifying witches are using their practice to strengthen and promote radical feminism. Some witches recently organized group spell casting via Twitter in an attempt to influence certain political leaders, but crowd-casting like that is still a novelty for now. The next generation of witches—digitally inclined and globally minded—may disrupt that too.

With the rise of the millennial witch, witchcraft as a brand also blew up, evidenced by the crowd of new shops (brick and mortar, but especially online) peddling witch-related wares and a general witchy aesthetic, spanning from crystals and herbs to tees and the ubiquitous enamel pins, and even spawning a rash of witch subscription boxes. But this app-savvy generation of witches also uses tech to share their discipline with the masses in creative and trendy ways, through dedicated witchcraft podcasts, in *Sabat*—a

sleek and moody biannual "magazine for the modern witch" (*Vice*, 2016)—and, of course, via social media.

Social apps, especially Instagram, significantly amplified witchcraft's visibility in the 21st century. Though some witches and Wiccans dismiss (and even despise) the craft's latest pop-culture commodification as a fashion trend, they can't deny its popularity. The biggest witch-lifestyle accounts continue to amass hundreds of thousands of followers, who increasingly are also potential customers—many of witchcraft's biggest Instagram influencers are proprietors of linked online shops. Still, even if only a small fraction of their social-media fans go on to research and espouse a form of witchcraft, it means more growth for the practice. At the very least, the popularity of these online accounts could help improve tolerance and acceptance of dedicated Wiccans and witches in real life, and possibly raise awareness in countries where relentless witch hunts and brutal executions remain a horrifying reality for vulnerable populations, especially women.

While pop culture's interest in witchcraft may ebb and flow—some say in 20-year cycles or during periods of social and political shifts—trends say that Wicca and witchcraft will continue expanding. Unfortunately, without a central organization to push for it, no one group is formally tracking the number of ceremonial witches—then again, the task would be truly Herculean when you consider the sheer volume of ways practitioners define witch and witchcraft.

Quantifying the number of practicing Wiccans isn't much easier. The Pew Research Center's 2014 Religious Landscapes Survey found that nearly 1 million people in the U.S. identified as "Pagan or Wiccan," up from about 140,000 in 2001 (according to the American Re-

NOOK OF SHADOWS
Above, a New York City magician rests in her conjuring room, which is crammed with more than 3,000 pieces of magical ephemera. Opposite, a modern witch.

ligious Identification Survey, conducted by the Graduate Center of the City University of New York). So while the practice of other religions is on the decline, the number of Wiccans rises, globally numbering, by some estimates, in the millions.

Given Western culture's long and violent history with witches, it's perhaps a bit surprising that neo-pagan practices like Wicca and witchcraft have found such a strong foothold in modern society. But by valuing individualism, celebrating nature and being flexible enough to evolve with societal shifts—sometimes even on the forefront of those changes—witchcraft does more than merely survive; it thrives, a contemporary tradition that, in one form or another, is also almost as old as time. ▲

A HERITAGE RECLAIMED

SALEM TODAY

More than 300 years later, the town of Salem Village,
now Danvers, has embraced its history

By Matthew Plunkett

For many years, even centuries, the legacy of shame, guilt and embarrassment about the witch trials kept the history of Salem Village (renamed Danvers in 1752) tucked away in the archives of various regional libraries. Playwright Arthur Miller discovered that during his 1952 visit, when, he observed, "you couldn't get anyone to say anything about it." That changed, though, with the birth of a witch named Samantha.

Samantha, as portrayed by actress Elizabeth Montgomery, was the lead character on ABC's television sitcom *Bewitched* (1964–1972) and, as the story goes, the descendant of one of the witches hanged at Salem. In 1970, ABC decided to film a number of episodes in Salem, and as if by magic, the spell prohibiting the town from owning its dark heritage was lifted. In the years that followed, the town of Salem fully embraced its past and hitched its economic future to the witch. Although not without some controversy.

Two years after the filming of *Bewitched*, the town of Salem created the Salem Witch Museum. The town also now boasts the Witch Dungeon Museum, Salem Witch Village and the Witch House. (As historian Stacy

VISITORS WELCOME
The Salem Witch Museum, open year-round, currently features an exhibition on the changing interpretations of witches, witchcraft today and the frightening phenomenon of witch hunting.

Schiff pointed out in a 2005 *New York Times* op-ed, the fact that the last of these structures, a home belonging to one of the judges in 1692, "neither belonged to an accused witch nor stood where it had in the 17th century" is beside the point.) Salem's police cars are adorned with silhouettes of broom-riding witches and Salem High School's sports teams are known, not surprisingly, as the Witches. Salem's enthusiastic embrace of its nickname "Witch City" is largely responsible for the 1 million tourists who visit the city each year.

In contrast with the kitschy appeal of a nearly year-round Halloween experience stands the Salem Witch Trials Memorial, a reminder that Salem's role in the worst mass panic in American history should not be forgotten. The architects drew inspiration from the Vietnam Veterans Memorial, and it stands in stark contrast to the statue erected in 2005, a nine-foot bronze statue depicting Samantha of *Bewitched* sitting astride a broom. Many longtime residents of Salem view the statue of a television witch as trivializing the ordeal of the 20 innocent victims who perished in 1692.

Salem has also, over the past 40 years, controversially evolved into an epicen-

SALEM WITCH MUSEUM

CHARTER STREET CEMETERY
The oldest cemetery in Salem contains four people connected to the trials: magistrate John Hathorne; physician Bartholomew Gedney; Mary Corey—first wife of Giles Corey, who was crushed for refusing to stand trial; Rev. Nicholas Noyes.

ter of New Age spiritualism. Over that time frame, a new interpretation has emerged that views witches as feminist icons and the 20 victims of the 1692 trials, particularly the women, as martyrs of an aggressively misogynistic society. Today, approximately 1,000 residents of Salem identify as witches. In the words of Erica Feldmann, owner of Hauswitch Home + Healing and dubbed the face of Salem's contemporary witch scene, "Witchcraft isn't about turning people into frogs, but being in touch with your 'inner power.'"

There is, of course, a measure of irony in contemporary witches' embrace of the history of Salem given that all 20 victims who lost their lives in the tragedy rejected that identity. Yet there is a common thread between these new witches and those accused of old: they are outsiders of one sort or another. Those accused of witchcraft often stood on the margins of society, either for reasons of age or economic standing or due to their norm-bending behavior. Women who spoke their mind or didn't live within the carefully drawn lines of societal norms often drew the unwanted attention of the witch hunters. Likewise, today's feminist witches find common ground with the witches of old. Historian Owen Davies, author of *The Oxford Illustrated History of Witchcraft and Magic*, writes that contemporary witches "rightly [see] social parallels between the past and present in terms of patriarchy and misogyny." Modern witches find comfort, solace and a safe place for self-expression through the medium of witchcraft.

Today Salem embraces all of its multifaceted history. Witch City boasts an almost perpetual Halloween experience, with all of its excesses. It is unabashedly kitschy in many respects, understanding the vital economic value generated from the town's identity with the popular conception of the witch. At the same time, the town draws in people seeking a different meaning from witchcraft. No longer associated with *maleficia* in the minds of these contemporary witches, the idea of the modern witch embodies a feminist philosophy in a still-male-dominated culture. Perhaps this latter segment of Salem does not account for the same level of economic activity as those individuals dressing in pointy black hats, but it says something about the inclusive and welcoming attitude of Salem that both populations feel accepted and welcomed. While the town entered history for its infamous executions of outsiders, Salem of the 21st century has evolved into a haven for people from all walks of life, no pointy hats required. ▲

SEVEN GABLES
This historic home in Danvers, formerly Salem Village, best known as the setting of Nathaniel Hawthorne's 1851 novel, was constructed for John Turner in 1668.

THE SALEM WITCH TRIALS

Editorial Director Kostya Kennedy
Director of Photography Christina Lieberman
Editor Alyssa Smith
Designer Allie Adams
Photo Editor Rachel Hatch
Writers Carina Chocano, Nancy Lambert, Daniel S. Levy, Matthew Plunkett, Alyssa Smith
Copy Editor Ben Ake
Reporter Gillian Aldrich
Photo Assistant Stephanie Durante
Editorial Production David Sloan

**TIME INC. BOOKS, A DIVISION OF
MEREDITH CORPORATION**
Senior Vice President, Finance Anthony Palumbo
Vice President, Marketing Jeremy Biloon
Director, Brand Marketing Jean Kennedy
Sales Director Christi Crowley
Associate Director, Brand Marketing Bryan Christian
Associate Director, Finance Jill Earyes
Senior Manager, Finance Ashley Petrasovic
Senior Brand Manager Katherine Barnet

Editorial Director Kostya Kennedy
Creative Director Gary Stewart
Director of Photography Christina Lieberman
Editorial Operations Director Jamie Roth Major
Manager, Editorial Operations Gina Scauzillo

Special thanks: Brad Beatson, Melissa Frankenberry,
Kristina Jutzi, Joseph McCombs, Kate Roncinske, Rich Shaffer

MEREDITH NATIONAL MEDIA GROUP
President Jon Werther
Meredith Magazines President Doug Olson
President, Meredith Digital Stan Pavlovsky
President, Consumer Products Tom Witschi
Chief Revenue Officer Michael Brownstein
Chief Marketing & Data Officer Alysia Borsa
Marketing & Integrated Communications Nancy Weber

SENIOR VICE PRESIDENTS
Consumer Revenue Andy Wilson
Digital Sales Marla Newman
Research Solutions Britta Cleveland
Product & Technology Justin Law
Chief Digital Officer Matt Minoff

VICE PRESIDENTS
Finance Chris Susil
Business Planning & Analysis Rob Silverstone
Content Licensing Larry Sommers
Corporate Sales Brian Kightlinger
Direct Media Patti Follo
Strategic Sourcing, Newsstand, Production Chuck Howell
Consumer Marketing Steve Crowe
Vice President, Group Editorial Director Stephen Orr
Director, Editorial Operations & Finance Greg Kayko

MEREDITH CORPORATION
President & Chief Executive Officer Tom Harty
Chief Financial Officer Joseph Ceryanec
Chief Development Officer John Zieser
President, Meredith Local Media Group Patrick McCreery
Senior Vice President, Human Resources Dina Nathanson
Executive Chairman Stephen M. Lacy
Vice Chairman Mell Meredith Frazier

PHOTO CREDITS

FRONT COVER Illustration by Tim O'Brien
BACK COVER Peabody Essex Museum/Bridgeman Images
TITLE PAGE Nina Leen/The LIFE Picture Collection/ Getty Images
CONTENTS Private Collection/Look and Learn/ Bridgeman Images

INTRODUCTION
P. 5: CPA Media—Pictures from History/Granger
P. 6: Leemage/UIG/Getty Images
P. 8: Granger
P. 9: © MGM, courtesy Photofest

PART 1: EUROPEAN ORIGINS
P. 10–11: Fine Art Images/Heritage Images/Getty Images
P. 13: Photo12/UIG/Getty Images
P. 14–15: Fine Art Images/Heritage Images/Getty Images (2)
P. 17: bildagentur-online/UIG/Getty images
P. 18: Mary Evans Picture Library
P. 20: DeAgostini/Getty Images
P. 21: Granger
P. 23: Interfoto/Bildarchiv Hansmann/Granger
P. 25: Bettmann/Getty Images
P. 26: Private Collection/The Stapleton Collection/ Bridgeman Images
P. 27: Universal History Archive/UIG/Getty Images
P. 28–29: Thomas Ernsting/Laif/Redux

PART 2: THE SALEM WITCH TRIAL
P. 30–31: American School/Private Collection/Peter Newark American Pictures/Bridgeman Images
P. 33: American School/Private Collection/Peter Newark American Pictures/Bridgeman Images
P. 35: Universal History Archive/Getty Images
P. 36–37: Private Collection/Bridgeman Images (2)
P. 39: Courtesy Everett Collection
P. 41: Granger
P. 42–43: Granger (2)
P. 44: Granger
P. 45: Nina Leen/The LIFE Picture Collection/Getty Images
P. 46: The Print Collector/Hulton/Getty Images
P. 49: Peabody Essex Museum/Bridgeman Images
P. 50: Briggs Co./George Eastman Museum/Premium/ Getty Images
P. 51: Omniphoto/UIG/Bridgeman Images
P. 53: Nina Leen/The LIFE Picture Collection/Getty Images
P. 54: (From top) Unimedia Images/REX/Shutterstock; Nina Leen/The LIFE Picture Collection/Getty Images
P. 55: Granger
P. 56: Nina Leen/The LIFE Picture Collection/Getty Images
P. 57: Historia/REX/Shutterstock
P. 58: Nina Leen/The LIFE Picture Collection/Getty Images
P. 59: Jerry Cooke/Pix Inc./The LIFE Images Collection/ Getty Images
P. 60: Jerry Cooke/Pix Inc./The LIFE Images Collection/ Getty Images
P. 61-65: Nina Leen/The LIFE Picture Collection/Getty Images (5)

PART 3: MODERN WITCHCRAFT
P. 66–67: Jens Meyer/AP/REX/Shutterstock
P. 69: Hank Walker/The LIFE Picture Collection/Getty Images
P. 70: Robert Phillips/The LIFE Images Collection/Getty Images
P. 71: Bettmann/Getty Images
P. 73: Nina Leen/The LIFE Picture Collection/Getty Images
P. 74: Paul Schutzer/The LIFE Picture Collection/Getty Images
P. 75: Gjon Mili/The LIFE Picture Collection/Getty Images
P. 76–77: © 20th Century Fox/Courtesy Everett Collection
P. 78: (From top) Mary Evans/Warner Bros. MGM/Ronald Grant/Everett Collection; © Buena Vista/Courtesy Everett Collection
P. 79: Courtesy Everett Collection
P. 80–81: (Clockwise from top left) © Viacom/Courtesy Everett Collection; © Columbia Pictures/Courtesy Everett Collection; Katie Yu/© The CW/Courtesy Everett Collection; Hulton/Getty Images
P. 82: © Warner Bros., courtesy Photofest
P. 83: (From top) Michele K. Short/© FX Networks/Courtesy Everett Collection; Robert Viglasky/SKY Productions/ Sundance Now
P. 85: Filip Singer/EPA/REX/Shutterstock
P. 86: Rick Loomis/Los Angeles Times/Getty Images
P. 87: Petras Malukas/AFP/Getty Images
P. 88: Stuart Griffiths/Camera Press/Redux
P. 89: Earl Wilson/The New York Times/Redux
P. 91: Elan Fleisher/REX/Shutterstock
P. 92–93: Berthold Steinhilber/Laif/Redux
P. 94: Carl D. Walsh/Aurora Photos

JUST ONE MORE
P. 96: Courtesy Everett Collection

ARE YOU A GOOD WITCH . . . OR A BAD WITCH?

The classic depiction of a witch reflects that of *The Wizard of Oz*'s Wicked Witch of the West: pointy hat, female, malevolent. The foundations for this portrayal were set long ago by the events of the witch hunts of the medieval era.

Made in the USA
Monee, IL
14 August 2020